31 DAYS TOWARD

Intimacy

with

GOD

JONI EARECKSON TADA

MULTNOMAH
BOOKS

31 DAYS TOWARD INTIMACY WITH GOD
Published in association with the literary agency of Wolgemuth and Associates, Inc.

© 2005 by Joni Eareckson Tada
International Standard Book Number: 978-1-60142-827-1

Portions of material previously published in *Secret Strength, Glorious Intruder,* and *A Quiet Place in a Crazy World*

Cover design by Kirk DouPonce/UDG Designworks
Cover image by Illustration Works

Unless otherwise indicated, Scripture quotations are from:
The Holy Bible, New International Version © 1973, 1984 by International Bible Society,
used by permission of Zondervan Publishing House
Other Scripture quotations are from:
New American Standard Bible® (NASB) © 1960, 1977, 1995 by the Lockman Foundation. Used by permission.
The Holy Bible, New King James Version (NKJV)© 1984 by Thomas Nelson, Inc.
The Holy Bible, King James Version (KJV)
The Living Bible (TLB)© 1971. Used by permission of Tyndale House Publishers, Inc. All rights reserved.
Holy Bible, New Living Translation (NLT)© 1996.
Used by permission of Tyndale House Publishers, Inc. All rights reserved.
The Message © 1993, 1994, 1995, 1996, 2000, 2001, 2002 Used by permission of NavPress Publishing Group
The New Testament in Modern English, Revised Edition (Phillips)© 1958, 1960, 1972 by J. B. Phillips
The Holy Bible, *English Standard Version* (ESV)
© 2001 by Crossway Bibles, a division of Good News Publishers. Used by permission. All rights reserved.
Contemporary English Version (CEV) © 1995 by American Bible Society

Published in the United States by Multnomah, an imprint of the Crown Publishing Group,
a division of Penguin Random House LLC, New York.

MULTNOMAH® and its mountain colophon are registered
trademarks of Penguin Random House LLC.

Printed in the United States of America

Library of Congress Cataloging-in-Publication Data

Tada, Joni Eareckson.
31 days toward intimacy with God / Joni Eareckson Tada.
p. cm.
ISBN 1-59052-002-5
1. Christian life—Meditations. 2. Devotional calendars. I. Title: Thirty one days toward intimacy with God
II. Title.

BV4832.3.T33 2005
242—dc22

2004026706

~

For Careen Peterson...
It's a joy to seek the heart of our Savior
every time we travel together!

Contents

Introduction

Smoothed and flattened, the wrinkled sheet of wide-lined tablet paper lay in the center of my empty desk.

A crayoned sun in the upper right corner beamed five thick rays onto the happy faces of dancing flowers. A white house with two large windows and red shutters sat squarely in the middle. In front of the house, sitting in a chair with large, spoked wheels, was a girl with blond hair, two pink circles on her cheeks, and a wide smile with neatly lined teeth.

I smiled. A portrait of me?

Big blockish letters scrawled with a red marker bore the following message:

DEAR JONI,
I LIKE MY CAT AND I LIKE SCHOOL.
WHEN I GROW UP I WANT TO HAVE A
WHEELCHAIR JUST LIKE YOURS.
LOVE,
SHANNON

My smile broke into laughter.

Shannon is a healthy, active little girl who plays hopscotch, four square, and "Mother, May I." She may not realize it now, but she has absolutely no use for a wheelchair.

Try telling that to Shannon! A wheelchair would top her birthday list, more coveted even than a purple bicycle with pink and white streamers on the handles. As far as she's concerned, a wheelchair means *adventure*. A joyride. An initiation into a very special club.

Shannon hasn't a clue about the price one actually pays to join such a club. The pain. The paralysis. The disappointment. The heartache and the hurdles. She discounts all that. She disregards the dark side, considering it not worth even knowing. All she desires is the chance to identify with me, to be like me, to know me. If that means having a wheelchair, then great—she'll take it!

It takes a child like Shannon to illuminate the meaning behind Paul's words to the Philippians:

> I consider everything a loss compared to the surpassing greatness of knowing Christ Jesus my Lord, for whose sake I have lost all things....
> I want to know Christ and the power of his resurrection and the fellowship of sharing in his sufferings, becoming like him in his death.
>
> 3:8, 10

There's no better way to identify with Jesus—to be like Him and to know Him—than to gain initiation into the fellowship of His sufferings. Or as Shannon might say, "the Club."

Suffering has a way of taking life out of the abstract, out of the theoretical, making it painfully concrete. Lofty sermons from eloquent Bible teachers don't bring release to people locked in suffering. Ph.D. programs in ivy-walled seminaries don't deliver hope and comfort to those in deep pain.

When we suffer, we realize we are not handling theological ideas, we are rather being handled by a Person—the warm and intimate Person of the Lord Jesus. At other times, when life is rosier, we may slide by with knowing *about* Him. With imitating Him and quoting Him and speaking of Him. But only in the fellowship of suffering will we *know* Jesus. We identify with Him at the point of His deepest humiliation. The cross, symbol of His greatest suffering, becomes our personal touchpoint with the Lord of the universe.

No one's asking you to beg membership in the Club as my little friend Shannon might. But there is something about her wonderful, wild abandon, her childlike trust, that must endear her to the Lord.

You don't have to choose suffering. You don't have to choose pain and humiliation. All you need do is choose God's will, as Jesus did on His cross. When you do, you'll be initiated into the Club—the fellowship of His suffering. And this is intimacy of the highest order.

Dear friend, since you've picked up this particular book and read this far, I think I know something about your heart. You have a longing to move toward a closer, deeper, more intimate walk with our God. That's what I want, too! More than anything. So why don't we agree to walk together for a while? Let's take a thirty-one-day journey toward the heart of heaven, and into the love of our Father and our Savior. Since we can never come to the end of His love, or truly understand the fellowship of His suffering, this little excursion represents only a few steps on the way.

Maybe so. But they will be steps in the right direction.

Day 1

REACHING FOR HIS HAND

This is a crazy world.

TV ads for luxury SUVs and sports drinks bookend stories of car bombings in Baghdad. A handicapped infant is left to starve to death in a neonatal unit, while a couple two thousand miles away search high and low to adopt a child—any child. Millions of dollars are spent to protect the eggs of birds on an endangered species list, while human babies are aborted in the third trimester. Battered wives paste on smiles as they dress for church. A preteen girl writes in her prayer diary, "My daddy took away my innocence last night."

It's all crazy.

I've seen the insanity and cruelty of man in places such as Bucharest, Manila, Quito…Auschwitz.

The madness began in Eden, where man and woman chose to part company with their Creator. Whenever man gains control, chaos and darkness reign. It is insanity that blights beauty, shatters peace, and brings hurt and injustice and cruelty and neglect. It is an insanity that preys upon the innocent and crushes dreams and quenches the light of hope in young eyes.

But this is still "My Father's World."

He shines in all that's fair;
In the rustling grass
I hear Him pass;
He speaks to me everywhere.

In His coming, the Lord Jesus hallowed this broken, crazy world. He breathed earth's air and felt the warmth of its sun and drank its cool water and walked its dusty highways. Earth's soil drank in drops of divine sweat, tears, and blood.

The Holy Spirit is here, the wise and gentle Counselor. He speaks through His Word, and He shines through the lives of countless believers all over the world.

It is a crazy world. We keep crazy schedules. Life speeds by at a blur. The crazy waves of circumstance roll over us, overwhelm us, threaten to drag us under.

Yet God is with us, no matter where we find ourselves in life. Right in the middle of the insanity. And anywhere, at any time, we may turn to Him, walk with Him, talk to Him, hear His voice, feel His hand, and catch—even if just for a moment—the fragrance of heaven.

Intimacy with God is an island of sanity in a sea of confusion. It is a quiet place, and it is *ours*. Whenever we look up into the face of our Father…whenever we reach for His hand…whenever we quiet our spirit to hear His voice…we have found a place of refuge and intimacy that nothing in this crazy world can take away.

A Step Closer

God is our refuge and strength,
A very present help in trouble.

PSALM 46:1, NASB

Please pray with me: Lord, even though I face a busy day

(or have just lived through one!),

even though I find myself running from this to that,

from here to there, I still want to crawl into the shelter of

Your arms. Even though my life moves at a blur,

I want to still myself in Your strength.

I want to rest in Your protection and tender care,

even when I feel like I'm wrestling alligators.

I take refuge in You, Jesus.

This day, all day, and all days.

Day 2

HE ALREADY
SEEKS YOU

God is an intruder.

He encroaches, presumes, invades, and infringes. He crashes the party. Tears aside curtains. Throws open locked doors. Hits the light switch in dark rooms. Pulls the fire alarm in stuffy, sacrosanct hallways.

He intruded primeval chaos and brought forth light, beauty, order, and life.

He presumed upon the life of a middle-aged man in the town of Ur, and brought forth a nation.

He trespassed on the cozy security of the Canaanites, smug behind their high walls of stone.

He advanced upon the lofty chambers of kings with feisty, finger-wagging prophets who called down judgment.

He was the unwelcomed guest at Belshazzar's feast, writing doom on the wall while the revelers gagged on their wine.

God intruded the womb of a virgin. He stormed Satan's kingdom on a Christmas night in Bethlehem. He talked out of turn in Judah and Galilee with words that "no man spoke before." He crashed the temple courtyards, overturning tables and kicking commerce out the door with a strong arm and a whip of cords.

God overstepped the realm of death itself, stealing its banner and crushing its lord. And in the Most Holy Place of the temple, He audaciously tore the veil from top to bottom.

And in the end, He will once again intervene in history, judging the nations, banishing sin and death, and setting His throne upon earth even as He rules in heaven.

God is a glorious intruder in my life, my thoughts, my pain, sorrow, and brokenness. The Spirit of the Lord even invades *me*, taking up residence in my very body. His Word is a razor-edged sword, piercing my complacency and dividing my soul and spirit. He boldly intrudes into my sin, calling it what it is, challenging me to leave it behind.

What can we do but marvel in speechless wonder at our powerful and almighty God—who, incidentally, has every right to intrude. After all, can the owner of the house really "intrude" when he sets his foot inside his own door? Can a king be tabbed "interfering" when he visits the subjects of his own realm? Can a craftsman be thought a "trespasser" when he puts a sharp knife to his own stick of wood?

God, an intruder? From His perspective, never. From our point of view? It happens all the time. Whether He encroaches with a gentle, "still, small" reminder or in sudden, devastating judgment.

And that's one reason why I have written this little book. So that you might understand that as you seek God, He is already seeking you. As you reach out for Him, He is already reaching for you. God cares enough to step into our lives...and sometimes when we least expect it. We dare not think that God is absent or daydreaming. He's not tucked away in some far corner of the universe—uncaring, unfeeling, unthinking, and uninvolved. Count on it, God wants intimacy with you more than you could ever desire intimacy with Him.

Thank His holy name that He intrudes in our lives!

A Step Closer

"You can throw the whole weight of
your anxieties upon him,
for you are his personal concern."

1 PETER 5:7, PHILLIPS

Day by day, hour by hour, moment by moment,
God monitors your thoughts, your concerns, your anxieties,
and the deep-down fears no one else knows but you.
He is not passive but active in your life,
whether you acknowledge His hand on you or not.
Invite Him into your thoughts, your plans,
and concerns, and, as He says in Revelation 3:20,
"I will come in."

Day 3

He Stoops to Bring Us Higher

Sometimes the thoughts that fill my head are anything but high and lofty.

Take last night for instance. After Bible study, a few of the girls hung around and started talking as we sipped coffee.

You'd think we would have discussed what we learned from the study, right? No. Instead we debated the pros and cons of laundry detergent sold in see-through plastic bottles so you can tell when it's near empty. Oh yes—and then we discussed how somebody ought to put a clear plastic strip on the sides of toothpaste pumps so you can tell when they're running low. Let's see…we discussed the sale at a local women's wear store, and why they decaffeinate coffee the way they do. Then we talked about news reports of what the first lady has been up to.

Little wonder God said to Isaiah, "For my thoughts are not your thoughts, neither are your ways my ways…. As the heavens are higher than the earth, so are my ways higher than your ways and my thoughts than your thoughts" (55:8–9).

Somehow, I don't think God stays up at night worrying about laundry detergent or lingerie sales.

But let's take a moment to let those verses from Isaiah sink in. God's thoughts are so much higher than ours we can't even begin to comprehend the gap that must be bridged. If we're to walk and talk and feel with our Father, it stands to reason we must begin to *think* as He thinks. "Do two walk together unless they have agreed to do so?" (Amos 3:3).

Somehow, my thoughts need to be conformed to God's—or else I cannot hope to know Him or become like Him as He desires. But what can I possibly do to rise to His level? To elevate my thinking? To think His thoughts? I can think as much as I please, but my thoughts—limited, finite, and so very human—still leave me on earth.

Ah, but all is not hopeless. Why? Because even though my thoughts cannot bear me up to the Almighty, *He* nevertheless is still thinking about me. The psalmist declares, "How precious are your thoughts about me, O God! They are innumerable! I can't even count them; they outnumber the grains of sand!" (Psalm 139:17–18, NLT).

Do you get the picture? God thinks about us. *He* bridges the gap. *He* makes intimacy possible. He makes His thoughts available. He puts His thoughts into words we can understand, stooping to make Himself comprehensible to a finite mind. In fact, His thoughts are what the Bible is all about. Praise His name, they *are* within grasp! And when we lay hold of Him and His ideas, then and only then can we be drawn closer to Him.

Take some time for that today. Open your Bible to a passage such as one of those I've mentioned—Isaiah 55 or Psalm 139. Invite His Holy Spirit to shine the light of understanding on everything you read. You may be surprised at how heavenly minded your thoughts really can be.

That's not only amazing, that's grace!

A Step Closer

Look deep into my heart, God,
and find out everything
I am thinking.

PSALM 139:23, CEV

"Who can know what the Lord is thinking? Who can give him counsel?" But we
can understand these things, for we have
the mind of Christ.

1 CORINTHIANS 2:16, NLT

God will not only enter our thoughts
(He is already there),
but He will order them, purge them of evil,
and draw them up to a higher plane so we can begin
to grasp spiritual realities beyond what we
could ever fathom on our own.
Invite Him into your inmost thoughts
once again today, and give Him freedom
to do His transforming work.

Day 4

THE PRICE OF INTIMACY

There can be no intimacy with God apart from repentance. And contemplating the kindness and goodness of God always leads us to repentance.

I was thinking about that a few days before last Easter. Like most of you, I read through the story of the

Crucifixion to prepare my heart for Easter morning. But I recall spending more than a few hours deliberating over the words of Christ when He cried in anguish from the cross, *"My God, my God, why have You forsaken Me?"*

I have to admit it. The idea that the Father would allow His Son to suffer the torture of crucifixion is beyond me. The humiliation of nakedness, the searing pain, the smell of blood and sweat, the agony of tears, the spit of drunken soldiers, the scorn of a laughing, jeering mob. When the crowd thinned and the cowards took shelter from the lashing storm, Jesus was left alone. As tears mingled with blood on His battered face, He cried aloud to His Father—the One who had not once turned away from Him in all eternity.

The reply was silence. Cold, accusing silence.

Heaven itself accused Jesus of sin in those horrible moments: lusting and lying; cheating and coveting; murder and hypocrisy; cruelty and deceit. Of course, Jesus had never been guilty of even one of those sins. *But we are.* And every one of your sins and mine was racked up on His account right there on that cross. The prophet testified:

Yet it was our weaknesses he carried; it was our sorrows that weighed him down.... He was wounded and crushed for our sins. He was beaten that we might have peace. He was whipped, and we were healed! All of us have strayed away like sheep. We have left God's paths to follow our own. Yet the LORD laid on him the guilt and sins of us all.

ISAIAH 53:4–6, NLT

Paul wrote:

He forgave all your sins, and blotted out the charges proved against you, the list of his commandment which you had not obeyed. He took this list of sins and destroyed it by nailing it to Christ's cross. In this way God took away Satan's power to accuse you.

COLOSSIANS 2:13–15, TLB

So where was God's goodness in treating Christ so? Where was the Father's kindness in turning His back on His only Son—while Jesus cried out in horror and grief?

On that terrible, wonderful day, God's goodness and kindness were directed toward you. God forsook His own Son, so that He would never have to forsake you! And because of those dark hours two thousand years ago, God can say to me, "I will never leave *you*, Joni, I will never forsake *you*."

This is the blood price of intimacy with a living, holy God.

As I pondered that amazing thought, I felt ashamed. The goodness of God was, indeed, leading me to repentance. To think that God's anger for my sins was poured out on Christ—and that He has no anger left for me.

You know what that makes me want to do? Praise Him. Thank Him. Honor Him. Obey Him with all my heart and soul and mind. Unlike Christ, I will *never* have to agonize over separation from my Father. And neither will you. God poured the full measure of His wrath—the terrors of eternal hell—on His own Son...so that you and I could be adopted into His very family. That's how much He loves you. And me.

His goodness has a marvelous way of pushing us to repentance.

A Step Closer

Do you show contempt for the riches of
his kindness, tolerance and patience, not
realizing that God's kindness leads you
toward repentance?

ROMANS 2:4

Pray the words of Psalm 51
back to the Lord today,
and receive a fresh start on the
way toward intimacy with Him.

Day 5

PULLING BACK
THE CURTAIN

I well remember the drudgery of Algebra 1 back in junior high.

I've never been the mathematical, linear, or logical type. Always motivated to dig into music, art, history, and English, I've relished math like a trip to the dentist. Sure,

I'd do my homework, study theory, listen in class, and try my hardest to understand what all my classmates apparently had little difficulty grasping. But somehow those funny little formulas never seemed to penetrate my gray matter.

But then came a day, a day still clear in my memory, when I discovered the truth of negative numbers. If you could have been sitting there in class with me, I just know you would have seen that big proverbial light bulb flash on over my head. Ah-hah! Eureka! I was thrilled to finally be able to grasp all those equations and proofs.

Discovering truth after a long mental wrestling match is an exhilarating experience. But we shouldn't make the mistake of equating that sort of intellectual discovery with the experience of grasping the truth of God's Word. We can participate in Bible studies, do our homework, grapple with all kinds of doctrines, and try really hard to make sense of Scripture. But if any light bulb flicks on in our understanding, it's probably not because we've "discovered" truth. More likely, it has been *revealed* to us. By God.

Peter thought he made a great discovery when he answered Jesus' question with the words, "You are the

Christ, the Son of the living God" (Matthew 16:16). In the
next verse, however, Jesus is quick to declare that it was
no artful detective work on Peter's part that brought him
to that all-important truth. Peter did not discover who
Jesus was. Christ said, "Blessed are you, Simon son of
Jonah, for this was not revealed to you by man [that is, by
human logic and surmising], but by my Father in heaven."

We can't unearth spiritual truth by the muscle of intel-
lect or the brawn of our brains alone. God the Holy Spirit
reveals these things to us. In fact, God goes so far as to
say He hides these things from the wise and intelligent,
revealing them instead to the childlike.

Perhaps our prayers today ought to be seasoned with
the kinds of petitions that simply say, "God, reveal
Yourself to me. Reveal Your truth in Your Word."

We may be surprised to find that all of our homework,
study, listening, and trying will be effective. Not because
we've put so much energy into it, but because our Father
in heaven has chosen to pull back the curtain.

A Step Closer

"Call to me and I will answer you,
and will tell you great and hidden
things that you have not known."

JEREMIAH 33:3, ESV

What an invitation into intimacy!
Call to Him today...not just once,
but over and over again.
He has given His children the awesome privilege
of walking in His Spirit.
Ask Him to open your eyes to
life situations as He sees them.

Day 6

A Picture of God

A little boy pulled out his crayons and sheet of paper one afternoon. Resting his hand on his chin, he thought for a few minutes, then picked up a crayon and began sketching.

Noticing his intentness as he worked, his mother asked, "What are you drawing?"

"A picture of God," he replied without looking up.

His mother smiled. "But honey, no one knows what God looks like."

The boy put down his crayon and rubbed his hands together, still staring at his handiwork.

"Well," he replied, "they will when I finish."

We smile at that little story. On one hand, we can understand the mother's point of view. John 1:18 tells us that no one has seen God at any time. God Himself told Moses, "You cannot see my face, for no one may see me and live" (Exodus 33:20).

Nobody knows what He looks like.

Yet even though none of us has ever looked God in the face, all of us desire to know something about Him, don't we? We drive up into the mountains, awed by the power displayed in His majestic creation. We sit by the seashore at twilight or early in the morning and listen for His voice in the roar of the waves.

We long to see God and somehow know Him.

Our heart longs for intimacy.

But even though Scripture reminds us that no one can look on the face of God at any time, that same verse goes on to declare that God's only Son, Jesus Christ, *has made Him known.*

To a bewildered Philip, Jesus replied, "Don't you know me, Philip, even after I have been among you such a long time? Anyone who has seen me has seen the Father. How can you say, 'Show us the Father'? Don't you believe that I am in the Father, and that the Father is in me?" (John 14:9–10).

Through His life and words and deeds, the Nazarene sketched an unerring illustration of His Father. He drew a picture so that we would have a clear idea of just who our Father in heaven really is.

No man has seen God at any time. Yes, that's true. Yet John tells us that the day will come when "we shall see him as he is" (1 John 3:2). Not in the reflected glory of a burning bush or pillar of cloud, but face to face. Until that time, however, God has already provided a revelation of Himself. Jesus Christ is that perfect expression of the Father. There should be no confusion, no questions. Our curiosity about God can be satisfied in Jesus.

You and I today are very much like that little boy

with his crayons. Through our words and deeds, our everyday conversations, and our attitudes and actions, we are sketching an illustration for all to see. Our lives should be a portrayal, a rendering, a picture of what God looks like.

If we remain intent on living for Him, people will approach us and ask what we're doing. They'll be curious. Looking over our shoulders. Maybe even asking questions. Hopefully, they'll see a beautiful image in us—a clearer picture of just who God really is and what He's like.

No, He's not finished with us yet. But Paul assures us that as we fix our gaze on the Lord Jesus, we will resemble Him more and more with each passing day. "We, who with unveiled faces all reflect the Lord's glory," he writes, "are being transformed into his likeness with ever-increasing glory" (2 Corinthians 3:18).

So let's pick up our crayons and get to work! We've got a job to do. We've got to show a despairing, cynical world what God really looks like.

And if they don't know before, maybe they'll know when we're finished...or, rather, when *He's* finished.

A Step Closer

"Here's another way to put it: You're here to be light, bringing out the God-colors in the world. God is not a secret to be kept. We're going public with this, as public as a city on a hill."

MATTHEW 5:14, *THE MESSAGE*

Would you pray with me?

Lord Jesus, strip away everything from my life that keeps Your life from shining through me in all its radiance and beauty. Help me to see all of my life — the happy and the sad, the full and the lean, the joyful and the painful, the peaceful and the perplexing — as a moment-by-moment opportunity to let this lost and broken world see You.

Accomplish it by the overflowing power of Your mighty Spirit.

In Your strong name, Amen.

Day 7

KEEPING GOD'S ATTENTION?

There's nothing more frustrating than trying to keep someone's attention.

I went through that game as an immature teenager, desperately seeking to impress the captain of the football team from our neighboring high school. I vividly recall those ridiculous mental gymnastics I went through…trying to dress right…combing my hair just so…losing those few extra inches around my waist…working so hard to impress…striving to pique his interest with my witty conversation. I felt that his fondness for me waxed and waned according to how clever and cool my overtures were.

What a disaster that relationship was! Frankly, I got plain worn out trying to hold his affection. He dumped me and I deserved it. Through it all, however, I learned something that's stayed with me through the years.

I'm reminded of that frenzied high school romance every time I catch myself trying to keep *God's* attention. Have you ever thought of it in those terms? When illness comes, when anxiety threatens, when conflict disturbs our friendships, we may conclude God has gotten bored (or worn out) looking after us, and has shifted His attention to a more "exciting" Christian.

"Look over there, Archangel Gabriel. Now, that young woman has possibilities. She's a climber. So responsive! So disciplined and faithful! On her way up in the kingdom. Too bad about Joni. I think we've invested more than enough time and energy in her for a while."

Or we imagine that God becomes disgusted with our meandering obedience and decides to stand us up, leaving us to fend for ourselves for a while. ("I'll teach *her* a lesson!") We're afraid that if we don't somehow keep ourselves in God's spotlight, He'll get too busy juggling galaxies or fulfilling prophecy in the Middle East. Or worse yet, we might so exasperate Him that He won't take the time to sort out the complicated mess we've gotten ourselves into.

If you ever find yourself thinking thoughts even remotely like these, run, don't walk, to the book of Psalms. Get alone for a few uninterrupted minutes with Psalm 121. Open your heart and let the Spirit of God bring those words home to you in a very personal way. It won't be long before those feelings of discouragement and inner turmoil begin to fade like a bad dream.

Down in a valley, in desperate need of encouragement, the psalmist looks all around him—north, south, east, and west. From where will his help come? Only from the Lord, the very creator of those intimidating mountains and hills that surround him (vv. 1–2). With his eyes focused on this mighty source of strength, the singer's spirit begins to bubble over with assurance.

This caring, concerned God, he tells us, "will not let your foot slip." Twenty-four hours every day, seven days a week, He will keep watch over you. He is a shade to you through long, weary days and a guardian through the darkest of nights (vv. 3–6).

Does anyone *really* care about your life? The Lord God does. "He will watch over your life." As a matter of fact, "the LORD will watch over your coming and going both now and *forevermore*" (vv. 7–8).

Oh, please don't make the mistake of supposing God's desire for intimacy with you waxes and wanes according to your spiritual temperature. God's love doesn't vacillate according to how many victories you have over sin or how many times you use His name in your prayers. His love for you goes deeper than mere affection or surface infatuation.

Your God will never be fickle. He will never give up on you. He will never become distracted. His interest will never cool with the passing years. You don't have to worry about trying to impress Him in order to catch His eye. In fact, His constant desire is to draw you closer into His embrace.

Read Psalm 121 and let the matchless love of God sweep away your doubts and fears. You already have God's complete attention, and you will never lose it. The real question is, how will He keep yours?

A Step Closer

But Zion said, "I don't get it.
GOD has left me.
My Master has forgotten I even exist."
"Can a mother forget the infant at her
breast, walk away from the baby she
bore? But even if mothers forget,
I'd never forget you—never.
Look, I've written your names on the
backs of my hands."

ISAIAH 49:14–16, *THE MESSAGE*

In Psalm 46, the Lord says,
"Be still, and know that I am God."
Another way of saying that might be,
when we aren't still, we forget that God is God.
We forget that He loves us, knows everything about us,
and never loses sight of us for a moment.
Do you have a place—and a space—away from the
noise and busyness of your daily world to just focus
your attention on Him…
and feel His unwavering attention on you?
Go there today.

Day 8

WOUNDED BY
THE WORD

*H*ave you ever read a verse scores of times and yet never had it affect you? Then you casually pass by it again and—*zap!*—it hits you squarely between your heart and mind.

There are times when you welcome the Spirit's intrusion. The new insight makes you smile. Out of nowhere you can see what God means. A bright new idea opens up.

At other times, there are no smiles at all. The new insight only brings a groan or tears. You're convicted of manipulating a friend. You're crushed over snubbing a new coworker. Shamed for gossiping about a neighbor. You've been wounded by the Word of God, and you have no excuse not to obey from then on.

Andrew Murray put it this way: "Jesus has no tenderness toward anything that is ultimately going to ruin a man in service to Him. If God brings to your mind a verse which hurts you, you may be sure there is something He wants to hurt."

That's the way God works. He is so very exacting. That's because He doesn't want us to see our disobedience vaguely or in general. Specific verses have a way of convicting us specifically.

It happened to me just the other day. I was reading through the third chapter of John and came across a verse I've glossed over at least 189 times. But on that day, the words of Jesus stung me like a whip: "Just as Moses lifted up the snake in the desert, so the Son of Man must be lifted up, that everyone who believes in him may have eternal life" (vv. 14–15).

It all started with an odd question from the Spirit: *Do you like snakes?*

Snakes? I hate them. They're repulsive. Disgusting. Detestable. I want to run away every time I see one. But what does this verse have to do with snakes?

You tell Me, I sensed the Spirit prodding.

Well, Jesus must have had a reason for using the words "snake" and "Son of Man" in the same sentence.

So…?

So I guess He was likening Himself to the brass serpent which Moses put on a pole—a serpent which mortally wounded people gazed upon in order to be saved.

So Jesus made Himself to be a serpent…a serpent of sin.

Jesus likened to a snake? Never! Snakes are too disgusting. Too…evil.

Ah, but Jesus BECAME sin for you. Just how do you think the Father looked at His Son—His Son who had become sin?

That's when it hit. It suddenly dawned on me why Jesus used a snake to describe His own pending crucifixion. When the Father turned His back on his Son, He was repulsed over the loathsome object of sin Jesus had become—a despised servant of sin. Little wonder God turned away from His Son, forsaking Him. Perhaps God felt the same way I do when I want to turn my back on a disgusting, repulsive snake, slithering along the ground.

Sin *is* loathsome, horribly offensive to God. And when I consider that my sin—individual, particular sins like snide remarks, deliberate exaggerations, prideful actions—drove such a wedge between the Father and His beloved Son on the cross...I am heartbroken. Overwhelmed. Humbled.

God wounded me with those verses from John 3. I'm sure there was something He wanted to hurt: my tendency to view disobedience as a vague generality. You see, I'm less likely to correct my disobedience when sin comes plain-wrapped as generic wrongdoing, obscure and ill-defined. I'm more likely, however, to correct my offense when the Spirit pinpoints a particular sin.

Our specific sins hurt Jesus specifically. Understanding what our disobedience did to Jesus, and seeing how our disobedience repulsed the Father, we should want to make certain we keep our lives pure. Doesn't it make your heart break? Overwhelm you? Humble you...just a little?

I hate snakes. I only wish I hated sin half as much.

A Step Closer

Search me, O God, and know my heart;
Try me and know my anxious thoughts;
And see if there be any hurtful way in
me, And lead me in the everlasting way.

PSALM 139:23–24, NASB

If there is a situation, practice, or habit in your life that consistently grieves the Spirit of God, you won't be able to find the intimacy with Him that your heart desires.

Use the above two verses as a starting point, and ask the "Searcher of hearts" to bring to your awareness anything that hinders your relationship with Him.

Day 9

OVER THE TOP

I had just finished packing my bags. Ken had packed his things, too, including his rods and reels. We had to be away from one another for several days, I on a speaking engagement, and he on a fishing trip. We knew we'd really miss each other.

Wheeling through the living room that afternoon, I

was surprised to see a beautiful red rose in a bud vase on the table. That Ken! So thoughtful. Moving into the bedroom to gather my things, I spotted another rose in a bud vase on my dresser. I was shocked. I glanced into the bathroom and to my amazement yet another red rose — a fresh, delicate little bud — adorned the counter.

By the third rose, I have to admit my excitement turned a little sour. It wasn't that I didn't appreciate his gifts, it was just that…well, both he and I were ready to leave. Nobody but Scruff, our miniature schnauzer, would be in the house to enjoy such lovely flowers. *Expensive* flowers at that, I pointed out.

Ken just gave me a big hug, melting all my protests.

As I went off on that speaking trip, I thought of the quality that marks the ministry of love. And that is its sheer *extravagance*. Love is extravagant in the price it is willing to pay, the time it is willing to give, the hardships it is willing to endure, and the strength it is willing to spend.

Love never thinks in terms of "how little," but always in terms of "how much."

Love gives, love knows, and loves lasts.

And that is what God has given to us. The quality that

marks the ministry of God's love for us is the sheer extravagance of giving His most priceless and precious gift...His Son. When the Father considered ransoming sinful, wretched men and women such as us, I don't think He thought in terms of how little He should give, but *how much*. Our hearts should—must—overflow with thankfulness and gratitude for all our Father has given. He has made the way open to intimacy with His great heart.

When I returned home from my trip, I got an added surprise. Those little buds were in full bloom, brightening my home with their extravagance...and a lingering fragrance of love.

A Step Closer

And I ask him that with both feet planted firmly on love, you'll be able to take in with all Christians the extravagant dimensions of Christ's love. Reach out and experience the breadth!...Rise to the heights! Live full lives, full in the fullness of God.

EPHESIANS 3:17–19, *THE MESSAGE*

How great is the love the Father has lavished on us, that we should be called children of God!

1 JOHN 3:1

Because He has poured His love into our souls —
up to the rim and brimming over! —
let that extravagant love splash on someone near you today.
Go beyond the expected — right over the top.
And do it as unto the God who has extravagantly loved you.

Day 10

A FRIEND WHO LISTENS

I was sitting at my friend's coffee table, wrestling with whether or not I should tell her about the depression that had gripped me for several days. I decided to open up. I told my friend I needed to share a problem. Did she have time to listen?

"Sure," she said, and promptly rose to retrieve a whistling tea kettle from the stove. As she poured, I took a deep breath and started to unfold my situation.

"Milk in your tea?" she interrupted.

"Uh, sure," I said.

"Now, what were you saying?" she asked, sipping her tea. I went on with my story. Midway, the phone rang. Her daughter called from the next room. "Mom! It's Dad at the office."

My friend sighed. "I'd better take that. I'll be right back."

I waited, occasionally glancing at my watch. The longer she took, the more my hurt festered. When she came back into the kitchen, she babbled on about her conversation with her husband, having completely forgotten ours.

"Shall I warm your tea?" she asked, before sitting down.

No, I didn't want any more tea. I just wanted her to listen. But at that point, I wasn't so sure I wanted to talk.

You've had it happen. You'll be going through a heartache or period of loneliness and you'll want to tell a friend. Your phone calls, however, are persistently interrupted—or never returned. Or worse, you've drawn a friend aside to describe some of the things you've been going through, and you get the distinct impression she or he is distracted, only half listening. You get little eye contact and only a few vague, mumbled words for a reply.

Longing for counsel, you ask for advice and receive a shrug of the shoulders or a pat on the back and a "cheer up, chin up," kind of reply. And you find yourself wondering, *Does anybody really care about what I'm going through? Will anybody listen?*

Jesus had the same thing happen to Him. In Matthew 20:17–28, He and His disciples were on the road to Jerusalem. It would be His last earthly journey. He knew full well what awaited Him at the end of the road. Betrayal. A shameful trial. Brutal torture. A bloody cross. A lonely death on a dark afternoon. The sins of the world, of all time, dumped on His shoulders. Broken fellowship with His Father. The dread of it must have weighed heavier on His heart with each step.

He stopped and turned to His friends. He poured out His heart to them, telling them exactly what was going to happen to Him when He passed through those city gates.

Talk about unkind ears! The disciples not only

ignored His troubled words, they turned right around and began arguing about who was going to be tops in the coming kingdom—who was going to get the head honcho job or the hotshot seat near the throne. Two of them even sent their mother over to Jesus to argue their case. Unbelievable!

No kind words. No helpful advice. No sympathetic ears or compassionate hearts. The disciples, distracted and called away by their own ambition, were only half listening.

That may be the loneliest part of loneliness. Knowing that no one else really understands—or even cares—what you're going through. Knowing that your burden of pain is yours alone. That's the way it is sometimes, isn't it? Friends won't always be there. Or if they are, they may not always see past the surface. Others may be busy—justifiably so—or simply unavailable.

And there you are, carrying it all by yourself.

Thankfully, Jesus has been through it, too. He understands. He, too, knows what it feels like to have friends who can't, or perhaps don't, always care. So He's the one who lends the sympathetic ear.

His eye contact never falters.
He will not be distracted from your cry.
His heart is with yours in the middle of your pain.

A Step Closer

There is a friend who sticks closer than a
brother.

PROVERBS 18:24

I no longer call you servants, because a
servant does not know his master's business. Instead, I have called you friends, for
everything that I learned from my Father I
have made known to you.

JOHN 15:15

I've never had a brother,
but I have that kind of friend in Jesus.
Read John 15:12–15, and ask yourself,
"What in friendship has He done for me?
And what does He expect of me as a friend to Him?"

Day 11

A FRIEND IN TROUBLED MOMENTS

I know my husband Ken almost (but not quite) like the back of my hand.

I'm not bragging, but honestly, there's hardly a feeling he can hide from me. I know that when his eyes narrow more than usual, he's worried. When his mouth stretches and his lips flatten in a certain funny way, he's irritated. When he spends too much time leafing through fishing magazines, he's depressed.

I also know there's not much Ken likes to keep hidden from me. He's the kind of guy who desires to be transparent, who invites me to know him on a deeper, more intimate level. And because I know Ken very well, I trust him. In fact, it's almost in mathematical proportion: The more I get to know my husband, the greater my trust in him.

When it comes to our relationship with God, this knowledge-trust formula is more than a matter of mathematics. It's a truth straight out of Scripture. King David put it this way: "Those who know your name will trust in you, for you, LORD, have never forsaken those who seek you" (Psalm 9:10).

It's cause and effect. A direct link. You can't have one without the other. To know God—to walk in true intimacy with Him—is to trust Him.

That should be good news if you've been troubled lately by a lack of trust, an inability to depend on the Lord through big or little problems. There *is* an answer. If you want to increase your resolve to trust God, to rely on Him faithfully, to depend on Him consistently, then you must seek to know Him better.

Paul the apostle understood that. He put Psalm 9:10 into his own words when he wrote: "I *know* whom I have believed, and am convinced that he is able to guard what I have *entrusted* to him...." (2 Timothy 1:12; italics added). As far as Paul was concerned, he could unquestioningly trust God with his health, his income, his ministry, his relationships, simply because he had grown intimate with the Lord.

So how can you find intimacy with God?

Seek. Look. Search. And be encouraged! Scripture declares that if you "seek the LORD your God, you will find him if you look for him with all your heart and with all your soul" (Deuteronomy 4:29).

That verse gives me the impression God is calling us to spend time with Him beyond what we ordinarily plan. Extra moments outside of our usual Bible study or quiet time. Ah, but I can almost read your thoughts: *Come on, Joni, get real. I have my quiet time each day, participate in a small group ministry, and have nightly devotions with my spouse. And now I'm supposed to make MORE time?*

Wait. It's not so much that we "make more time" for Him. It's more a matter of recognizing that *all* of our time is His.

Imagine, for instance, that you're slumped on the couch watching a mindless sitcom on TV. During a commercial, the Spirit whispers, "Turn it off and spend a few moments with Me." What's your response?

Or let's say you're tossing and turning in bed, fretful that you can't get to sleep. Out of nowhere the Spirit interrupts your anxiety with a quiet suggestion: "Why don't you use this time to pray?" Do you?

Or maybe you have a choice between a new magazine that's just come in the mail and your favorite devotional book. The Spirit intervenes, suggesting, "Let's spend time together in that devotional you haven't picked up in a while." Which will it be?

God loves to break in beyond the bounds of the structured minutes we've scheduled for Him. To be honest, those are often the times where real intimacy with God begins. Trust can only increase when we redeem those

precious, inopportune, untimely moments as ways to
know Him better.

A Step Closer

When my anxious thoughts
multiply within me,
Your consolations delight my soul.

PSALM 94:19, NASB

In the verse above, did you notice when the psalmist

experiences God's comfort and companionship?

Right in the middle of an anxious day—

square in the midst of a sleepless, worry-torn night.

The Holy Spirit waits to flood your soul with His hope

and joy—even in your most troubled, pressure-filled moments.

Ask Him to do that today.

Day 12

FINISHING TOUCHES

It was my first recording session. I had studied for days, memorizing all the melodies. But what really excited me was the thought of hearing it all put together—violins, piano, horns, and harps. All the tracks blending into one beautiful expression.

To get an idea of how it was done, I went down to the recording studio several days in advance, just to listen to the musicians lay down the orchestral background music. They gathered in a little studio, representatives of the musicians union, some of the top professionals in the country.

The arranger put the score sheets down before them and—believe it or not—after one rehearsal they were ready for a take.

I was stunned that these people could just walk right in and play a very complicated score—full of sharps and flats, minor and descant chords—all on sight. The sound they created was breathtaking. Absolutely beautiful.

But do you know what happened after they went through it once and got it down on tape? Many of them left their seats and went on break, milling around the rooms of the recording studio, sipping on Cokes or coffee. They seemed totally detached from the beauty of the music they'd just had a part in creating. Only one or two bothered to listen to the playback.

I couldn't believe it! How could these people create something so extraordinary and then...just walk away from it, not wanting to hear its final form?

Since that experience, I've thought about God's joy in creating something beautiful in us. Philippians 1:6 tells us that, "He who began a good work in you will carry it on to completion until the day of Christ Jesus."

In other words, He will develop that good work that He has begun in your heart and life. He will perfect it and bring it to a full and satisfying completion.

You see, God doesn't walk away from His creation. He doesn't take coffee breaks. He's not off relaxing somewhere between jobs, sipping on some refreshments. He's never nonchalant or aloof about the work of His hands. He's creating something beautiful in us—far more beautiful than a symphony.

For Him it's not simply another job that needs to be done. His reputation is at stake and His Son's image is the model. It's perfection that God has in mind—maturity in Christ, that's the end result.

God is always finding new ways of refining you and changing you and improving upon the score He's written with you in mind. He's at work in your life today. He's not on a break, no matter what your faltering faith or weary emotions might tell you. Even in seasons of suffering and pain, He draws out deeper, more beautiful chords than anyone imagines, blending them into your life symphony.

He's going to stick around. He's going to be there for the finishing touches. When it comes to the tracks of your life, He's going to be involved with the blending and sorting. And on the day of Christ Jesus, He'll be there with you for the playback. All of heaven will be stunned to see and hear what His marvelous work has created in your life.

A Step Closer

For those God foreknew he also predestined to be conformed to the likeness of his Son.

ROMANS 8:29

Let's just take a moment to pray....
Abba Father, thank You for Your assurance that every life
experience—no matter how perplexing or heartbreaking—
is making me more and more like Your own Son.
No experience—no matter how senseless it might seem—
is wasted. The shaping hurts sometimes, Father,
but by faith I affirm that the end result will be glorious.

Day 13

YIELDING TO HIS TOUCH

He began his career as a jockey—a wiry, short, but very strong boy from Italy. It didn't take long for him to make a name for himself around the stables and among the top owners. After jockeying a number of blue-ribbon Thoroughbreds, he went on to become a master horse trainer. You could ask most anybody around Baltimore's Pimlico racetrack back in the 1940s. Pop Trombero was one of the best.

By the time I met Pop in the mid-1960s, he had long since retired from the track. Actually, Pop became family…my sister's father-in-law. At various family gatherings, Pop would come to our farm and go horseback riding with us.

On one such occasion I recall my sister asking me to let Pop ride my horse, Tumbleweed. I protested. Listen, that horse was *mine*, and I didn't want anyone else riding her—even if he was an "expert." After a few minutes, however, I felt ashamed and gave in. I watched Pop Trombero tighten his jockey saddle on Tumbleweed as I saddled one of the older, slower horses. While we rode, I stuck close to Pop and Tumbleweed—just to make sure he didn't jerk on her bridle or tug at her reins.

After a few minutes on the trail, I realized I had nothing to worry about. In fact, observing the way Pop handled my horse, I grudgingly realized I had a few things to learn. He was so *tender* with Tumbleweed. Constantly talking to her. Continually stroking her neck. Always giving her his undivided attention. No matter how interesting the trail, Pop's focus never diverted from that horse for a moment.

You wouldn't believe the way Tumbleweed responded. She became a different horse! Her ears pricked up. She listened to his commands, never balked, obeyed instantly. It seemed her joy to do Pop's bidding. I was amazed! I looked down at my mount, realizing I'd hardly paid any attention to the animal. And the way my horse acted, it showed.

Wonderful things happened when a master like Pop touched a horse. He knew how to guide. He knew how to bring out the best. And wonderful things happen when the Master touches our lives as well. Mark 6:56 tells us that "as many as touched him were made whole" (KJV).

His attention never diverts from you for a moment. His touch in your life is constant, unchanging, always tender.

Is it the joy of your life to do His will? To obey? To pick up your pace when you feel His nudge? To slow down at a gentle tug on the reins?

The Lord God knows how to guide you as no one else. He knows how to bring out your best.

Intimacy with God is really a matter of yielding to the Master's touch.

A Step Closer

I will instruct you and teach you in the
way you should go;
I will counsel you with my eye upon you.
Be not like a horse or a mule, without
understanding, which must be curbed
with bit and bridle,
or it will not stay near you.

PSALM 32:8–9, ESV

In what area of your life are you resisting the Master's touch?

Has He revealed that to you?

Pray for the grace to yield — to release —

in that area and ask Him to guide you along

the path of His choosing.

Day 14

THE LITTLE THINGS

Is God concerned about the details of your life? Does He care about the "little things"?

Maybe you've shaped words like those in your heart—if not on your lips—during the course of a busy day at home or the office. Piles of dishes need to be loaded. The

washer leaks a big soapy puddle on the floor—and you've
got guests coming in an hour. Your best friend seemed cold
on the phone, and you can't figure out why.

Little things.

Nobody else seems to notice or pay that much
mind...so why should God? After all, isn't He the God of
the big things? Isn't He the One who spoke swirling
galaxies into the vast frontiers of space? Isn't He the One,
as Isaiah wrote, who

> Has measured the waters in
> the hollow of His hand,
> And marked off the heavens by the span,
> And calculated the dust of the
> earth by the measure,
> And weighed the mountains in a balance
> And the hills in a pair of scales?

40:12, NASB

Why should this great, awesome God notice the tears
that came to my eyes this morning at breakfast—when no
one else noticed? Why should the Creator of the universe

care about the worries that kept me awake until 2:00 a.m.? Why should the mighty Sovereign of eternity be concerned about the fact that I'm late for an appointment and can't find a parking place?

Sure, the Bible says He has compassion for His people. But isn't that sort of a "general" compassion for mankind? Isn't that an arm's-length kind of compassion? Like a multimillionaire might feel when he writes out a check for an anonymous poor child living on the other side of the world.

Just how intimately is God involved in our small, petty problems?

Again and again I go back to David's words in Psalm 103:

> Just as a father has compassion on his children,
> So the LORD has compassion on those who fear
> Him.
>
> V. 13, NASB

This verse gives us an idea just how and in what way God expresses His compassion. It isn't the compassion of a distant king...or a distracted executive. The kind of compassion God has is the intimate, heartfelt compassion of a *father*.

I remember my father having that kind of compassion with me. Often when my dad would be busy at his easel, mixing oils and painting on his big canvas, I'd be sitting on the floor at his side with my crayons and coloring book—working just as hard as he was. And even though he was intent on his work, he'd look down at me and smile. And sometimes he'd set his brushes aside, reach down and lift me into his lap. Then he'd fix my hand on one of his brushes and enfold his larger, stronger hand around mine. Ever so gently, he would guide my hand and the brush, dipping it into the palette, mixing the burnt umbers and raw siennas and stroking the wet, shiny paint on the canvas before us.

And I would watch in amazement as, together, we made something beautiful.

I look back on that scene, even these many years later, and find myself warmed by the intimate, emotional compassion my father had for me.

This is the kind of love our God has for us! Fatherlove. The kind, gentle compassion of a dad who deeply cares for his sons and daughters. Maybe you never had a dad like that, but you do have such a Father.

No, God is not so preoccupied with the running of His big universe that your problems and concerns—even the little ones—somehow escape His notice. The Lord Jesus assured us that "even the very hairs of your head are all numbered." So if your problems today are piling so high that you feel ready to stumble beneath the weight of them, stop and take Peter's good advice to "cast all your anxiety on him because he cares for you" (1 Peter 5:7).

Let God's big hand close gently over yours. With His help, even the discouraging crayon scribbles of your life can become a masterpiece.

Nothing would delight a father's heart more.

A Step Closer

You keep track of all my sorrows.
You have collected all my tears
in your bottle.
You have recorded each
one in your book.

PSALM 56:8, NLT

Can you imagine a God who keeps track

of every tear you have ever shed since infancy?

(Remember, it says He has collected all our tears.

Every one of them.)

He has been there in every sorrow and

disappointment you have ever experienced.

Praise Him today for His tender love and watchful care!

Day 15

"LISTEN, LISTEN TO ME..."

*M*y computer has company this morning. But then, it has company every morning. A Bible rests on top of the CPU. A hymnal leans companionably against the monitor. A well-thumbed *Book of Common Prayer* lies within easy reach on a shelf above. On a lower shelf, flanking the keyboard, a book of Christian poetry props up against a volume on the name of Jesus.

These are tools that help me listen to God.

As in anyone's day, I'm constantly shifting gears from one task to the next. But I dare not rush between jobs without pausing to thank God for what was just completed…and to ask Him for guidance on what is to be done next.

That means pausing to listen. That means raising my spiritual antennae to discern His clear directional signal.

How do we do that here at the office? Maybe Francie and I will flip open a hymnal and harmonize on "My Faith Looks Up to Thee." Or we'll grab a coworker on her way to the copy machine as she passes by the office door, and have her join us on a verse of "Great Is Thy Faithfulness." We'll take a minute to consider one of the names of Jesus. *Counselor. Word of God. Bread of Life. Ancient of Days.* Then maybe we'll take a long sip of coffee, hold hands, and pray…which always includes keeping "ears tuned" to what the Lord thinks ought to be accomplished in the next task, whether it's an article or a letter or part of a manuscript.

You might call it priming the pump. I call it listening to God. I listen for His voice. I wait. I take the time. And He has never failed to meet me at that place of listening. He gives me instructions. Impressions. Convictions. Directions. Gentle rebukes. Affirmations. Whether I turn to the right or to the left, my ears hear a voice behind me, saying, "This is the way; walk in it" (Isaiah 30:21).

Don't turn back, He tells me. Don't turn aside. Come straight ahead, and I will be with you.

It's the same in my painting studio. I wheel into the room, and the illustration board stares back at me. Big, blank, white, scary. It's intimidating. It's frightening. I sometimes feel suddenly weak, or dull, as if I could never come up with another idea as long as I live.

"O God," I whisper, "help me! What do I do? What do You want me to do?"

And in the quietness of my little studio, I do very much the same as in front of my blank computer screen. I read some Scripture. Sing a hymn. Murmur a prayer. Listen to some classical music. Leaf through some big art books, letting my eyes linger on the works of the masters. Surround myself with color. And then…listen. I just listen for His voice. I wait to see where He wants me to begin, what He wants me to do.

I wheel back away from the easel, so I won't be tempted to charge in and start throwing paint around prematurely. I let the room become very, very silent. And wait. And wait. Until I hear something. And then I say, "Yes, *yes*. Of course. That's the way I want to begin. This is the way it should be."

Waiting for God to speak can be stretching at times. In different places around the world, I have been backstage waiting for my introduction and really not certain of what I was supposed to say. Days before my speaking engagement, I ask Him again and again, "What do You want me to communicate here? What do these people need to hear from You?" As the engagement draws near and He doesn't tell me, it gets tense. And there have been times—an hour before I have to speak—in my hotel room, when I cry out to Him, "But Lord, You haven't told me yet what You want me to say."

Yes, the answer comes. It always has. The words are there when I need them. But not always when I *want* them!

To listen in prayer is to mentally absorb divine instructions concerning the matters of the day. To listen—*to find true intimacy with your God*—is to not take the day in one fell swoop, but in hourly or even moment-by-moment increments. The day's schedule which looked organized in the morning can, like a deck of cards, be shuffled by noon. Circumstances can shift. Plans can change. That's why keeping your heart's ear cocked hour by hour is so important.

Listening implies confidence that God truly desires to speak with us. Only as we learn to hear the voice of the Father can we learn to shut our ears to the voices of the world.

It's always easy to hear our own voices, because we are basically selfish people. But it's a matter of tuning—fine-tuning the ear of the heart—to discern God's desires and intentions.

You cannot have intimacy with heaven apart from this firm determination to listen for God's voice. It means, as Scripture says, *inclining your ear* to what He has to say, just as He inclines His ear to our prayers. I sometimes imagine a little girl pulling on her dad's trouser leg. And that big man gets down on his knees and looks into his little daughter's eyes, and says, "I'm listening. What is it, honey?" If that's the way God listens to my voice, I want to hear every word that He has to say, too.

Our usual tendency is to march into prayer with our own agenda, assuming that whatever is on God's heart will for certain match what's on ours. To be honest, our tendency is not even to be concerned about His heart's desire for our prayer time—hence, our lack of interest in listening.

We cover over His voice with a lot of noise and frenzy and motion. We hear the Holy Spirit speaking a quiet word to our heart, but then finish His sentence assuming we've caught His drift. Or receive His message but are too busy or too distracted to make sense of it. We tell ourselves we'll go back and double-check it later, but by the time we get around to it, the moment is gone. The voice is silent. The opportunity is passed.

For many of us, prayer has become a one-sided, one-dimensional recitation of our needs and wants and thoughts. And yes, it's true, He loves to hear us speak. But He also loves to speak in return.

That's the way it is with intimate friends.

A Step Closer

"Everyone who listens to the Father and learns from him comes to me."

JOHN 6:45

"The friend who attends the bridegroom waits and listens for him, and is full of joy when he hears the bridegroom's voice."

JOHN 3:29

"Listen, listen to me, and eat what is good, and your soul will delight in the richest of fare."

ISAIAH 55:2

Add a half hour to your time with the Lord today—and dedicate it to quieting your heart and listening for His voice. If the weather allows it, go for a walk and ask Him to walk with you and speak to you.

Day 16

HANDHOLDS IN
HIS CHARACTER

As I was emerging from my depression over being paralyzed, I uncovered a promise in the Bible about God's faithfulness. Philippians 1:6 told me to be confident, in fact, of this one thing: That He who had begun a good

work in me would carry it on to completion until the day
of Christ Jesus.

You have to put that promise in the context of my life
at that time. For the first time since my accident, I was
trying to peer into my future. Yet it seemed as though a
thick, black curtain hung just inches in front of my face.
The appalling reality of a *lifetime* of paralysis was almost
more than I could bear. My faith seemed paralyzed, too. It
was hard to imagine how anything good would come out
of it—ever. I was convinced I would never smile again.

But then I came across Philippians 1:6.

Like a drowning woman clutching a life preserver, I
immediately grabbed hold of the faithfulness of God. I
took hold of His tenderness and mercy. I quoted the verse
to the Lord, asking Him to fulfill His promise of complet-
ing a good—yes, a *very* good—work in my life.

And do you know what? I found peace. I was confident that God, in His faithfulness, would hold Himself to
His promise.

Charles Spurgeon once said, "You and I may take
hold at any time upon the justice, the mercy, the faithfulness, the wisdom, the long-suffering, the tenderness of

God, and we shall find every attribute of the Most High to be, as it were, a great battering-ram with which we may open the gates of heaven."

Obviously Spurgeon wasn't talking about "nuking" the gates of heaven to somehow overcome God's reluctance or unwillingness. No, God is not an immovable meditating mystic who has to be prodded to perform His will. Spurgeon isn't talking about God that way. But I do think that it pleases God when we seek His glory, His will, even His character in a given situation in our lives.

Abraham, pleading with God to spare Sodom, reminded the Lord, "Shall not the Judge of all the earth do right?" (Genesis 18:25, NKJV). Did God need a reminder? "Oh, thanks, Abe. I'd completely forgotten that angle. Thanks for jogging My memory." Obviously, God did not need a nudge to remember His justice. Yet He was delighted that Abraham sought heavenly justice on the merits of the heavenly Judge. Abraham pleaded his case from the platform of God's character.

Habakkuk, too, appealed to God's very nature in his prayer. It was a time of deep national distress in Judah. The ruthless Babylonian army was poised to sweep across

the country like water from a ruptured dam. Yes, the
prophet agreed with the Lord, Judah was deserving of
His judgment. But how could God use a people even more
evil than they as His rod of discipline?

> Your eyes are too pure to look on evil;
> you cannot tolerate wrong.
> Why then do you tolerate the treacherous?
> Why are you silent while the wicked
> swallow up those more righteous than themselves?
>
> HABAKKUK 1:13

David pleaded God's character again and again.
Discouraged by his own sins and unfaithfulness, he cried
out: "Remember, O LORD, your great mercy and love, for
they are from of old. Remember not the sins of my youth
and my rebellious ways; according to your love remember
me, for you are good, O LORD" (Psalm 25:6–7).

Intimacy with God involves finding handholds and
footholds in His character. Do you plead with Him on the
basis of who He is? Consider again His justice, His mercy,
His faithfulness, His wisdom, His purity, His might, and

His tenderness. If you're hurting or if you're confused, find some attribute of your great God and grab on to it with all your might, asking Him to deal with you accordingly. Humbly hold Him to His promise. God is delighted when you seek His will, His character, His glory—and yes, His heart—in your prayers.

A Step Closer

But you, O LORD, be not far off;
O my Strength, come quickly to help me.

PSALM 22:19

When David's strength was at its lowest ebb,

he cried out to the One who is Strength.

Where is your greatest point of need today? For strength?

Mercy? Purity? Wisdom? Love? Call out to Him,

and cling to that very attribute of His character. You will find

all that you need…and more than you could dream.

Day 17

EYE CONTACT

When I was a little girl, I remember secretly opening a small chest that belonged to my mother and taking out her diary. I don't remember if I was even old enough to read—and I certainly didn't learn anything shocking about my mom. But I do remember that panicky sense of excitement as I hid behind the living room piano and delicately turned each page as though it were forbidden treasure.

After finishing, I carefully placed the diary back into the chest, situating it just so. I went out to play, the whole time thinking about what I had done—and feeling worse and worse about seeing her at dinnertime.

Mom rang the dinner bell at the back door, and we kids came running. I busily filled the supper table with a lot of anxious chatter, trying hard to act normal.

Finally Mom asked what the matter was. And do you know something? I couldn't look her in the face. She'd catch my eyes for a moment, and then I'd quickly look down at my plate. Guilt prevented me from looking straight at my mother and answering her questions.

That little story is repeated in the lives of thousands of children and millions of adults. Looking one another straight in the eyes has always been a test of truthfulness.

God knows that. In 2 Chronicles 7:14, He says, "If my people, who are called by my name, will humble themselves and pray and seek my face and turn from their wicked ways, then will I hear from heaven and will forgive their sin and will heal their land."

How I love that verse. But especially the part about seeking God's face. Just as I had to make things right with my mom before I could have eye-to-eye contact with her, I have learned that God wants me to seek His face in the same way. He desires to have eye-to-eye contact with me—transparent, truthful, lacking any guilt, guile, or sin. But that means confessing sin—my responsibility. No use filling my prayers with a lot of anxious chatter, trying to fake it with the Lord or lie to myself.

If you have a hard time gazing straight into the face of the Lord today, then you know you've got some confessing to do. God wants you to seek His face. There's nothing like eye-to-eye contact with our loving Father.

A Step Closer

Finally, I confessed all my sins to you
and stopped trying to hide them.
I said to myself, "I will confess my
rebellion to the LORD."
And you forgave me!
All my guilt is gone.

PSALM 32:5, NLT

Read Psalm 32:1–7. Now, go back and pray those words to

the Lord (just as you did earlier with Psalm 51).

Take note of the Lord's kind and loving reply in verses 8–9.

What is the promise in these verses?

What is the warning? Never doubt it,

He is directing those words to YOU.

Receive them today as His encouragement and instruction.

Day 18

JUST JESUS

Years ago, Ken and I had the privilege of attending the funeral of Corrie ten Boom. It was a simple service. Brief, not many flowers, very European. But, oh, how challenged we were when we left the church that day.

Several pastors spoke about Corrie's life and work,

reading excerpts from her books or recounting incidents from her ministry. They all talked about her love of Jesus. One pastor said she had specifically instructed him to speak about the love of Jesus—*not* about Corrie ten Boom.

It was the same every time I visited with Corrie or heard her speak. Jesus was always at the center of her thoughts and words. She rarely spoke of "the Christian walk" or "the Christian experience." She didn't speak of Christ as though He were some creed or doctrine or lifestyle. She spoke about a Person. A Person she loved more than anyone else in the world.

As Ken and I left the graveside, I remarked that Corrie's life reminded me of Paul's words to the Corinthians: "When I came to you, brothers, I did not come with eloquence or superior wisdom as I proclaimed to you the testimony about God. For I resolved to know nothing while I was with you except Jesus Christ and him crucified" (1 Corinthians 2:1–2).

"How is it," I said to Ken, "that we get so caught up in explaining our walk in Christ, or life in Christ, or some spiritual experience—instead of simply talking about Him?"

I find myself going on and on about my testimony, my trust, my obedience, or "the God of the Bible." I talk more about details and doctrines than I do about Jesus, my Savior and Lord.

I wonder if you find yourself in a similar situation. God forbid that we should reduce our Savior to fine-print doctrines squeezed between the pages of a theology textbook. And may the Lord wake us out of spiritual slumber if we catch ourselves making a big deal of our "life in Christ" rather than the simple testimony of Jesus. May we never rely on clever techniques or catchy stories or that manipulative kind of speech Paul spoke of to the Corinthians.

Let's let the life of Corrie speak to us today. So often she would say, "Jesus is Victor!" Let Jesus be our message. Let Jesus be our hope and joy. *Let's seek intimacy with Him above everything else in life.* And let's tell people about that intimacy and love…just for Him.

A Step Closer

"He must become greater and greater,
and I must become less and less."

JOHN 3:30, NLT

Yes, everything else is worthless when
compared with the priceless gain of knowing Christ Jesus my Lord. I have
discarded everything else, counting it all as
garbage, so that I may have Christ and
become one with him.

PHILIPPIANS 3:8-9, NLT

Let's pray together.

Lord Jesus, forgive us if we've drifted into a careless,
cultural Christian walk. We talk about Christian books,
Christian political action, Christian music,
Christian bumper stickers, and Christian this and that,
and sometimes, Lord, leave You right out of the picture.
Bring us back, Savior, to a simple love for You
and a burning desire to know You, obey You,
please You, and watch daily for Your return.

Day 19

WHEN THE WORDS WON'T COME

Immediately after church on Sunday morning, a young woman with cerebral palsy approached me in her wheelchair.

CP is usually characterized by paralysis, weakness, or loss of coordination due to brain damage. Sometimes there are uncontrolled movements and slurred speech. This woman's speaking was especially difficult to grasp. She kept repeating a certain sentence over and over again. Even though I patiently asked her to repeat each word one by one, I still couldn't understand. The expression on her face gave me no clues at all. I couldn't tell if she was in terrible trouble or was simply trying to relay some profound experience.

Finally, after many attempts, I was able to piece her sentence together. She was asking me to help her find someone who could assist her to the restroom!

It was such a simple request. But I felt helpless, so inadequate that it had taken me so long to understand her need. Once it dawned on me what she was requesting, I moved quickly to get her help!

Can you imagine the hardship of not even being able to make your needs known? Wouldn't it be sad if there was no one around who could even understand you?

Ah, and yet that is the very predicament you and I find ourselves in. Listen to the words of Paul: "In the same way, the Spirit helps us in our weakness. We do not know what we ought to pray for, but the Spirit himself intercedes for us with groans that words cannot express. And he who searches our hearts knows the mind of the Spirit, because the Spirit intercedes for the saints in accordance with God's will" (Romans 8:26–27).

There are times when we want to talk to God but somehow just can't manage it. The hurt goes too deep. Fear locks our thoughts. Confusion scatters our words. Depression grips our emotions.

I'm so glad—so very, very thankful—that God can read my heart and understand what's going on, even when I am handicapped by my own weakness for words. As it says in Hebrews 4:13, "Nothing...is hidden from God's sight. Everything is uncovered and laid bare before the eyes of him to whom we must give account."

Words are not always necessary. When we are in such trouble we can't even find words—when we can only look toward heaven and groan in our spirit—isn't it good to know that God knows exactly what's happening? And when we face suffering...locked in physical pain, torn by grief, or pierced through with emotional wounds...when all we can do is fall before Him and cling to the edge of His robe, I am so humbled to know the Spirit of God prays for me with an eloquence no man or angel could match. The faintest whisper in our hearts is known to God. Even if it should be a sigh so faint that you aren't even aware of it yourself, He has heard it. And not only heard it, but He understands it—right down to the slightest quiver registered in our innermost being.

You and I may certainly be handicapped when it comes to understanding the groans and sighs of one another. And others—even those closest to us—may never be able to hear or interpret our deepest sorrows and longings.

But the One who searches hearts knows and understands. The Spirit is never handicapped by our weakness for words.

Praise His name! Our heavenward groans and wordless sighs have a voice before God.

A Step Closer

Let us then approach the throne of grace
with confidence, so that we may receive
mercy and find grace to help us in our
time of need.

HEBREWS 4:16

Sometimes—especially when we are suffering—
the only thing we can do is to approach the throne of grace,
as we have been invited, and kneel in silence before our God.
We may do so even when we can't put two words together in
prayer. The Bible promises mercy and grace in those times of
trouble and distress. His favor wraps around our shoulders
like a warm blanket, and His Spirit prays for us in words
beyond our comprehension. Step into that throne room right
now, and experience intimacy with your God.

Day 20

SHARP KNIFE IN A
LOVING HAND

When we used to go camping with my parents, my elderly father—now with the Lord—was a wonder to watch. While others busied themselves with tents and stoves, ice chests and lanterns, Daddy would slip quietly into the surrounding forest and begin gathering chunks of wood.

He would come back to the campsite with an armload—trunks of gnarled redwood, juniper, perhaps some pine that had had time to harden in the weather. Piling this trove near a comfortable rock, he would sit down, pull out his knives, and begin whittling away the crusty bark and dead, dry twigs, scraping off the dirt, moss, and any soft or decayed wood.

Sometimes, people who passed our campsite wondered why this little old man was so captivated by pieces of dirty, gray wood. Yet he worked on with deliberation, obviously with something very special in mind.

I often wondered at Daddy's work myself. Some of the pieces he selected looked utterly unredeemable. The weather had blasted and twisted them. Insects had gnawed and ravished them.

But Daddy worked on and on...and before you knew it, there was a mound of bark, dirt, and twigs piled at his feet. And in his grip, clean and shiny from the oils in his hands, and smooth from the cut of his knife, he would have shaped a lovely carving. It always amazed me to see the beautiful grain in the heart of that wood after the bark and decayed wood had been chipped away. Often, those lovely pieces would then be shaped into lamps, tables, chests, or stools.

Once while watching Daddy at his work, I did some work of my own—a charcoal sketch of him toiling away with his knife, cutting into a piece of wood. I entitled the rendering, "My Father's Creation."

Our heavenly Father is hard at work, too, creating something beautiful in the lives of His children as He shapes us with the knife of His Word. The Holy Spirit peels away the crusty, dead layers of our old nature. He cuts out the decayed areas of habitual sin and lops off the dead or dying branches that don't produce fruit. Slicing away at disease and damaged layers, His work reveals a changed heart, beautifully transformed by His sharp Word and His skilled hands.

There isn't one of us who doesn't feel the encrusted weight of our old nature. We long to have stubborn sins stripped away, and the worthless preoccupations and dead, earthbound things sloughed off.

God in His Word can do that. Yes, the cut of the knife

will be sharp, often painful. In our foolishness and fear we may even want to cling to some of those dead, fruitless branches. We may resist the suffering that He allows into our lives, wondering if He has forgotten about us. But God works on with deliberation, obviously with something very special in mind.

Christ Jesus in you.

A Step Closer

His powerful Word is sharp as a
surgeon's scalpel, cutting through
everything, whether doubt or defense,
laying us open to listen and obey.
Nothing and no one is impervious to
God's Word. We can't get away from it —
no matter what.

HEBREWS 4:12–13, *THE MESSAGE*

Are you more like Jesus this year than five years ago?

One year ago? Last month?

Make sure you have a regular reading

plan to be in the Bible every day—prayerfully, carefully—

allowing the Holy Spirit to gradually carve

and shape you to resemble the King of kings.

Day 21

IN THE PRESENCE
OF LIGHT

I was a child who was scared of the dark.

I didn't like being the first one through the front door to flick on the lights. And things didn't change much even after I became a teenager. I'd come home from a date and dread to see the house dark. Turning the key in the front lock and creaking open the door, I'd call, "Anybody home?"

I'd step into the hall and gasp—was that a man standing behind the living room sofa? On went the lights! Whew…it was only a lampstand. And that awful shadow looming outside the window was only the branch of a tree.

In the dark, shapes take on eerie silhouettes. True meanings are obscured. We're frightened by the unfamiliar.

But what a comfort light is! Light reveals things for what they really are. That lampstand was no threatening stranger. That tree shadow was no Peeping Tom. Light takes away the frightening guesswork. It makes reality clear.

As we read Scripture, we realize that it didn't take God very long to "turn on the light." In the second verse of the Bible, the author describes a brooding, primordial darkness. But in the very next verse, God says, "Let there be light."

As I pondered that statement recently, comparing it with other verses in Genesis 1, I discovered that God wasn't talking about the light of the sun, moon, and stars.

God didn't form the light-bearing heavenly bodies until later, on Creation's fourth day.

So what could He mean? Where was the light coming from? I checked a couple of cross references and noted this verse in John 1:

> In the beginning was the Word, and the Word was with God, and the Word was God.
>
> v. 1

It reminded me of a story I once heard Kay Arthur share. God is ready to begin Creation. The script is written; the play is about to commence. The curtain is closed, the stage is empty, and there's darkness all around. But God, much like the director of a great, moving drama, begins the play. *"Let there be light,"* He shouts, and the central character of Creation steps out to take the leading role.

Jesus, the Light of the World, the Creator and Sustainer of creation, walks out on stage in the middle of His own spotlight.

What a thought! How thrilled I was to see Jesus, the

Alpha and Omega, as described in the last book of the Bible, spotlighted in the very first book of the Bible.

Truly, God's Word begins and ends with Christ.

Where is He in your life today? Is He at the beginning of your day—and the end? Is He on center stage, in the spotlight of your plans, goals, and ambitions? Are you reading His script or somebody else's? Studying His Word or books about His Word?

He who is the Light of Creation now says, "You are the light of the world." He has given you and me the responsibility to reveal reality in a dark, sin-blinded world—to show things for what they really are.

People are afraid in these days of warfare and terrorism. People are confused, bewildered, and in despair as the last moral foundations of our nation crumble. It's time for the children of light to draw as near as we can be to the Source of all light.

Let it shine.

A Step Closer

The darkness is passing and the true light is already shining.

1 JOHN 2:8

Remember, our Message is not about our-selves; we're proclaiming Jesus Christ, the Master.... It started when God said, "Light up the darkness!" and our lives filled up with light as we saw and under-stood God in the face of Christ, all bright and beautiful. If you only look at us, you might well miss the brightness.

2 CORINTHIANS 4:5–7, *THE MESSAGE*

Do you remember the old luminous watches?
If you held them up against a light bulb for a minute or two,
then turned out the lights, the hands on the watch
and the dots by the numbers would glow brightly for
twenty or thirty minutes…and then fade.
It's the same with you and me.
The more time we spend in the presence of the
Light of the World, the more we will glow when we
move into the darkness of this broken world.
Take time today—in the midst of the busyness—
to step into His presence and bask in the
most beautiful light of all.

Day 22

JESUS KNOWS;
JESUS UNDERSTANDS

When we think of the trials and temptations of the God-man, we usually think of His wilderness experience. His desperate hunger and fiery thirst. Or that darkest of hours when His friends abandoned Him. We remember He had no place to call home. We recall He walked hundreds of weary miles. His muscles ached and His feet blistered. He cried real tears. And when they pinioned His body to that rough wooden cross, He not only bore our sins, but He *became* sin for us. He identified with every area of our human weakness.

But that profound identification didn't start with His public ministry. No, when I think of the extent Christ went to probe the depths of human experience, I think of His birth.

Even as a baby He identified. No pastel-papered, hygienic nursery for Him. No brand-new crib and changing table. No disposable diapers and baby powder. No musical mobiles of giraffes and teddy bears. No cotton swabs and baby ointment. No pink and blue needlepoint hanging on the wall. And those strips of cloth that covered His infant body were a far cry from Carter's top-of-the-line.

Right from the beginning of His journey on earth, the Lord sympathized with our weaknesses. He entered history in a smelly stable with a handful of hay for a pillow. The only music He heard may have been the muffled strains of a lyre and flute from the crowded inn nearby. The first fragrances to fill His nostrils were musty straw and animal manure. His first bed was a feed trough. His first changing table was a dirt floor.

Not one of us can ever point an accusing finger at Jesus and say, "You live in an ivory tower. You don't know what it's like!"

Maybe God planned it that way to make a point. Perhaps our heavenly Father wanted us to understand that in weakness there is strength. In poverty, riches. In humiliation, dignity.

Even as a baby, the Lord Jesus had a mission. Before He could even speak, His life was a message. His birth, in many ways, was a sermon. From the very beginning, He was demonstrating the extent to which divine love would reach.

This is the High Priest to whom we give our praises — during the Christmas season and all year long. This is the One we adore and to whom we sing our thanksgivings. We have a Savior who sympathizes with our weaknesses.

"Let us then approach the throne of grace with confidence" (Hebrews 4:16).

Because Jesus knows.

Because Jesus understands.

History and heaven defy anyone to say otherwise.

A Step Closer:

Therefore, holy brothers, who share in the heavenly calling, fix your thoughts on Jesus, the apostle and high priest whom we confess.

HEBREWS 3:1

For we do not have a high priest who is unable to sympathize with our weaknesses, but we have one who has been tempted in every way, just as we are—yet was without sin.

HEBREWS 4:15

Do it now. Fix your thoughts on Jesus.
Wonder at the enormity of the mission He undertook
to purchase our salvation. Marvel that He would go to
such lengths — not only to rescue us, but to be there for us,
a faithful and sympathetic High Priest, in times of
temptation and trial. Praise Him for becoming our great
High Priest, who pleads our case before the Father.

Day 23

THE COMFORT OF THE SPIRIT

A very special grandmother recently related the following experience to me:

> My daughter's call from the hospital emergency room shocked me. My granddaughter Robin, just

turned six, had fallen from the high bar at school, severely injuring her mouth. I picked up her sisters at school and spent a hectic, tense afternoon supervising the little ones while awaiting my daughter's return with Robin.

The doctor had taken eight stitches inside her mouth and six on the outside. As the little ones swarmed over their mother, Robin sat squarely in the biggest chair in the living room. Her face puffed almost beyond recognition, her long hair still ropy with dried blood, she looked tiny and forlorn. Still, I approached her cautiously, for Robin is the least demonstrative, most private of children.

"Is there anything you want, darling?" I asked.

She looked me firmly in the eye and said, "I want a hug."

Me too! I thought as I cuddled her on my lap. *But how and whom does an exhausted grandmother ask?* As we rocked gently, the words of Scripture came to me from John 14:16: "I will pray the Father, and he shall give you another Comforter, that he may abide with you for ever" [KJV].

So I asked, just as simply and plaintively as
Robin had asked. And just as simply, I felt His
everlasting arms enfold us.

Like that grandmother, we often long to have comforting arms surround us in our weariness, heartache, and
confusion.

That's what I love about the Holy Spirit.

Certainly, the Bible names Him as our Counselor. And
yes, He is our Intercessor. We're told elsewhere He is our
Teacher, Guide, and the Spirit of Truth. He reminds us of
everything Jesus has said. He reveals the Father. He even
convicts us of sin. He does so many things. But the one
thing I love most...

He's our Comforter.

There are times when I so yearn to feel the presence of
God I almost weep. And I know it is at those times the
Holy Spirit is earnestly praying for me. What a comfort to
sense His presence in such a close and personal way!

The Lord Jesus tells us in John 16:14 that the Holy
Spirit will only bring glory to Him. How true that is.
When I sense the consoling presence of the Spirit, it

makes me want to praise Jesus all the more.

He has a ready embrace for hurting little girls, heart-sick grandmas, worried daddies…and you, too, by the way.

You say it's been quite a while since you've sensed that holy hug?

Maybe it's been quite a while since you asked.

A Step Closer

But you, beloved, building yourselves up on
your most holy faith, praying in the Holy
Spirit, keep yourselves in the love of God.

JUDE 1:20–21, NASB

If you're hurting today, don't immediately

grab the phone to call a friend.

Seek the everlasting arms of the Spirit.

He is many things, but most importantly to you today,

He is your Comforter.

Day 24

GOD'S PURSUING
LOVE

When I stumbled headlong into my first big trial as a new Christian, I wondered just where the love of God had gone.

People spoke of God's love helping them through the hard times, yet I couldn't shake an absurd mental image of Him leaning against some ivory wall in heaven, casually thumbing in the direction of the Cross. "That says it all," I imagined Him saying.

I soon discovered I wasn't alone in that attitude. I've talked to a number of people over the years who imagine a bored, lethargic God…a God only passively interested in our circumstances—and slightly irritated if pushed to demonstrate His present-day love. Some describe Him as little more than a cosmic warehouse clerk, filling mail-order prayer requests. Others feel God abandons them when some other, "more obedient" Christian catches His attention.

My perception of Him has changed, of course, as I've grown in my faith. But even those of us who view Him as a powerful, caring God easily underestimate the strength of His determined love.

God does not observe our lives at a cool distance. He is neither apathetic nor detached. He is on the move. He is involved.

Listen to Andrew Greeley….

Our God is not patiently standing by and waiting for us to offer love; He is actively and vigorously pursuing us.… He is the father running down the trail to embrace the prodigal son even before the boy can speak his act of contrition. He is the mad farmer showering a full day's wage on men who hadn't even worked. He is Jesus forgiving the sinful woman even before she spoke her sorrow. He is the king lavishing a banquet on beggars. These are all symbols of a God whose love for us is so active, so strong, that by human standards He would be, at least, said to be mad.

God is not the sort to casually murmur, "Well, sure I love you." He constantly shows us how much.

Consider the impact we could have on our world if we began to pursue God with some of the intensity with which He seeks us! If we would respond in obedience the instant we discerned the Spirit's prodding. If we, like God, had a passion for holiness. If we would freely pour out our love as He does.

In a day when it's fashionable to appear cool, bored,

uncaring, and detached, we can't afford to doubt the enthusiastic, all-encompassing love of God. *And get a little excited about it.* His compelling love surrounds us every minute. He's in front of us, behind us, relentlessly pouring His love into our lives. What madness! What a passion for our souls! How can we be halfhearted in our circumstances toward others—when He loves us so?

May we be found running down the trail to forgive those who offend us. May we shower our abundance on those who don't deserve it. May we embrace the sinner before he even speaks his sorrow. May we be found praising and worshiping Him with all our hearts—without a single thought for "what others might be thinking."

A Step Closer

My soul followeth hard after thee: thy right hand upholdeth me.

PSALM 63:8, KJV

*What would it mean for you to wake up in the morning
and determine to pursue God with all your heart that day?
What would you do differently?
How would you "follow hard" after Him,
even in the midst of necessary routines?
Set your heart this day to pursue Him,
remembering how He is
(at this very moment) pursuing you.*

Day 25

TOUCHED BY
THE SPIRIT

The Carpenter must have paused in the conversation, feeling a cool evening breeze touch His face, tug at His robe. He may have gestured toward the dark shape of a nearby tree, listening to a murmur of leaves.

"The wind," He told the Pharisee, "blows wherever it pleases. You hear its sound, but you cannot tell where it comes from or where it is going. So it is with everyone born of the Spirit" (John 3:8).

I've always loved that illustration. Maybe it's because I've always loved the wind.

I think of a summer afternoon…relaxing underneath an old, wide-armed maple, watching the wind gently bend the branches and rustle the leaves.

I think of camping in a grove of pine trees…listening to the wind whistle and whisper through the forest.

I think of a November nor'easter…roaring across rain-wet fields in wild and wonderful fury.

I think of the smell of wind…bearing the fragrance of distant blossoms; the aroma of a cherrywood fire; the sharp, salt tang of the sea.

Little wonder Jesus likened the wind to the Spirit. Wind, by its very nature, *moves*. Just so, the Spirit never lies dormant, never stays within the soul. He's always moving, always making His presence known. And if this Holy One truly lives at the center of our lives, we will see…feel…at times almost smell and hear the effects of

His activity. The Spirit will constantly be *doing* something within us, something others will be able to observe.

Although we cannot see the wind with our eyes, we know it moves among us by the effect it has on trees, flowers, ocean waves, smoke from fires, ripples on a pool, waving wheat—and by its touch on our faces.

In the same way, you will know the Spirit lives in you or a fellow Christian by the effect He produces in character, conduct—and on our very countenance.

It's absurd to suppose you can have the Spirit of Christ within you and *not* see, feel, and experience His presence. The Holy Spirit *will* produce holy living. Paul says in Galatians 5:22 that "the fruit [or evidence] of the Spirit is love, joy, peace, patience, kindness, goodness, faithfulness, gentleness, and self-control."

The wind marks its movement by what it touches. And in its wake it leaves freshness and cleansing. As you allow the Spirit to fill and empower your life, others will mark His presence, breathe deeply of His fragrance, and give thanks.

A Step Closer

Because you are sons, God sent the
Spirit of his Son into our hearts, the
Spirit who calls out, "Abba, Father."

GALATIANS 4:6

If you have any encouragement from being
united with Christ, if any comfort from his
love, if any fellowship with the Spirit, if
any tenderness and compassion, then make
my joy complete by being like-minded,
having the same love, being one in spirit
and purpose.

PHILIPPIANS 2:1–2

Jesus said that the Father delights to give the
Holy Spirit to those who ask Him (Luke 11:11–13).
Being filled to overflowing with God's
Spirit isn't all that complicated.
You just have to ask—and then keep on asking,
with all your heart, every day of your life,
to be filled afresh. And you can start right now.

Day 26

A Place at the King's Table

Those of us who love God's Book find people we can identify with in its pages.

Strong, mission-minded believers find a champion in

the apostle Paul. Young pastors feel a strong kinship with Timothy—a green pastor with a problem church and a queasy stomach! Single girls swoon over Ruth's love story. Harried homemakers identify with Martha—but long to be more like her sister. Teens see themselves in the youthful David on his lonely, nighttime vigils. If children don't picture themselves with the little ones who gathered at Jesus' feet, they may sympathize with young Samuel, who had to leave his mom and dad to live in the temple.

I don't know too many stories of people in the Bible with spinal cord injuries. But there is one name I do remember from my Sunday school days—one disabled individual with whom I can identify.

Mephibosheth, son of Jonathan.

Prince Jonathan had died in battle along with his father, King Saul. Before his death, the prince and the fugitive David had been the closest of friends—though by all logic they should have been bitter rivals. When David ascended to the throne after the death of Saul and Jonathan, he wondered how he might honor the memory of his dear friend. So he summoned Saul's former household servant to the palace.

The king then asked him, "Is anyone left from
Saul's family? If so, I want to fulfill a sacred vow
by being kind to him."

"Yes," Ziba replied, "Jonathan's lame son is
still alive."

"Where is he?" the king asked.

"In Lo-debar," Ziba told him. "At the home of
Machir."

So King David sent for Mephibosheth —
Jonathan's son and Saul's grandson.
Mephibosheth arrived in great fear and greeted
the king in deep humility, bowing low before
him.

But David said, "Don't be afraid! I've asked
you to come so that I can be kind to you because
of my vow to your father Jonathan. I will restore
to you all the land of your grandfather Saul, and
you shall live here at the palace!"

Mephibosheth fell to the ground before the
king. "Should the king show kindness to a dead
dog like me?" he exclaimed.

And from that time on, Mephibosheth ate

regularly with King David, as though he were
one of his own sons.

2 SAMUEL 9:3–8, 11, TLB

It's no easy thing to be disabled, even in today's world. But it was immeasurably more difficult in those days. Not only was medical care all but nonexistent, but the disabled person had to endure the ceaseless stab of pity and prejudice. Believe me, nobody cared about accessibility back then! People who were lame or blind were either relegated to back bedrooms or forced to beg on city streets.

This was the kind of future faced by Mephibosheth, whose feet were lame. But all of that changed when King David found the young man and summoned him to his throne. Lame, considered worthless, an embarrassment even in his own eyes, the son of Jonathan was bidden by the king to come and dine.

As a former heir to the throne, Mephibosheth's expected fate would be banishment at best—and most likely death. And now the new king wanted to dine with him? What had Mephibosheth done to deserve this unprecedented honor?

Absolutely nothing.

When the disabled man asked the king the reason for this extraordinary compassion, David explained, "I will surely show you kindness for the sake of your father" (9:7).

It was because of David's great love for Jonathan that Mephibosheth was welcomed into the king's presence. Disability or no, he was now part of the family and enjoyed all the privileges of a king's son.

Isn't that the way God deals with us? We were alienated, crippled by our sin. Our disability was our ignorance and apathy toward the God who had every right to snuff us out in His righteous anger. As Paul put it, "You were spiritually dead through your sins and failures…and obeyed the evil ruler of the spiritual realm…being in fact under the wrath of God by nature, like everyone else" (Ephesians 2:1–2, Phillips).

Like Mephibosheth, the best thing we could have expected from our King was permanent banishment or a swift execution. But no. Because of Jesus, we are invited to become the very sons and daughters of God.

In love he...adopted [us] as his sons through
Jesus Christ, in accordance with his pleasure and
will—to the praise of his glorious grace, which he
has freely given us in the One he loves. In him we
have redemption through his blood, the forgive-
ness of sins, in accordance with the riches of God's
grace that he lavished on us....

Consider the incredible love that the Father
has shown us in allowing us to be called "children of God"—and that is not just what we are
called, but what we *are*.

EPHESIANS 1:4–8, NIV; 1 JOHN 3:1, PHILLIPS

Through Jesus' provision, we can now draw our
chairs up to the King's table. We are welcomed. In spite of
our spiritual disabilities—whatever they are—we are part
of a family. There is no reason to fear. The King has called
us into His intimate family circle as His own sons and
daughters.

Remember that, if today you feel unworthy to come
into the King's presence...if, like Mephibosheth, you sense
that somehow you could never fit in.

Come anyway, says the King. No matter what your weakness, handicap, or disability.

Come and dine.

A Step Closer

Consequently, you are no longer foreigners and aliens, but fellow citizens with God's people and members of God's household.

EPHESIANS 2:19

That I may gain Christ and be found in him, not having a righteousness of my own that comes from the law, but that which is through faith in Christ—the righteousness that comes from God and is by faith.

PHILIPPIANS 3:8–9

Grace, grace, God's grace,
Grace that will pardon and cleanse within
Grace, grace, infinite grace,
Grace that is greater than all my sin.

The old hymn says it well.
Our God's undeserved favor toward you and me is great —
in fact, infinite. He has not only invited you to His table
and adopted you into His very household circle,
He has deposited the awesome, unspeakably glorious
righteousness of His own Son into your account!
Praise Him today for His kindness and grace.

Day 27

THE SHADOW OF HIS WINGS

There's nothing like the furnace blast of dry heat that rises off the surface of the Arizona desert. I was only ten years old, and my cow pony and I had become separated from the rest of my family during an afternoon roundup on my Uncle Ted's ranch.

The air sizzled. Even when I strained my eyes, searching the horizon for the others, the distant images only wavered like a mirage. I kicked my pony in the direction of a huge, red boulder. Wiping my brow with my hat, I climbed down to find shelter in the shadow of the rock. Out of the blinding glare, my eyes relaxed. I took a deep breath of the cooler air. It was, for me, a place of refuge.

That shadow was also a place of safety and refreshment as I twisted my hat, praying that someone would find me. Only thing was, I had to keep inching over to the left to keep up with the shifting shadow. It was a fickle friend. I didn't mind too much, though. I was just relieved to picture myself, small and insignificant, huddling in the comforting shadow of what felt like almighty God. It was easier to pray because I felt protected and sheltered.

Within an hour I heard galloping hooves just over the dusty ridge. My family! And just in time. The changing shadow of the rock was about to disappear.

Shadows. Always moving.

Like Jonah crouching under the gourd vine, like a

worried little cowgirl huddling against a desert boulder, we find shadows fickle friends.

Ah, but our Lord casts an unchanging shadow!

James 1:17 tells us that, "Every good and perfect gift is from above, coming down from the Father of the heavenly lights, who does not change like shifting shadows."

That shadow never shifts, because our Father never changes. He's not "evolving," as some theologians would have us believe. He's not transmutable, as other religions profess. No, He is constant and changeless. Always compassionate. Always merciful. Always just. Always holy. Always full of love. Always there.

The shadow of a mighty Rock, within a weary land.

The relief we find in His presence, the delight we find in an intimate relationship with Him, does not change with the passing of the hours, days, or years. The encouragement we find in His promises will not fail us when the heat of adversity bears down upon us. The security we find in His character will never vary though our lives turn upside down and the world changes around us. And when we find ourselves in a season of deep suffering, He moves in even closer. As David wrote (and he ought to know),

"The LORD is close to the brokenhearted and saves those who are crushed in spirit" (Psalm 34:18).

How wonderful to have His shadow fall across us. Psalm 91 begins by saying, "He who dwells in the shelter of the Most High will abide in the shadow of the Almighty" (NASB). The psalmist goes on to detail the many ways God protects His own, making them feel secure. In verses 11–12 we're told, "For he will command his angels concerning you to guard you in all your ways; they will lift you up in their hands, so that you will not strike your foot against a stone" (NIV).

Psalm 121 assures us that:

He who watches over you will not slumber;
indeed, he who watches over Israel
will neither slumber nor sleep.
The LORD watches over you—
the LORD is your shade at your right hand;
the sun will not harm you by day,
nor the moon by night.
The LORD will keep you from all harm—
he will watch over your life.

vv. 3–7

If we are willing to place our lives in His hands and our faith in His Word, He will richly reward us by making the passing of each day's shadows a sign of His blessing to come.

You may fail Him—you *will* fail Him. But He will never fail you. Place your chair in the shadow of the Cross, and you will never have to move it.

A Step Closer

Because you are my help,
I sing in the shadow of your wings.
My soul clings to you;
your right hand upholds me.

PSALM 63:7–8

"I the LORD do not change."

MALACHI 3:6

Someone has said, "Lord, it can get awfully dark
under the shadow of Your wings."
And it's true. Our circumstances may become very bleak,
our skies may be socked in with a cloud cover so
heavy we think the sun will never shine again.
But over it all—over life, death, and eternity—
His wings overshadow and protect us.
We are His, and He will care for His own.
Take time today to meditate on Romans 8:18–27.

Day 28

A LIVING PATH TO THE FATHER

When you think about the Trinity, God the Father, Jesus the Son, and the Holy Spirit, to whom do you relate best?

I know what you're thinking: *It's a trick question —
they're all the same.* You're right, but I know many of us
relate to the different Persons in the Trinity in different
ways.

I heard of a woman, for example, who was terrified of
God the Father. She read all about Him in the Old
Testament, how He commanded His leaders to destroy
entire towns, how He slammed down an angry fist against
sin, how He demanded a high and holy standard. She
couldn't relate to God the Father, much less praise Him.

But, she said, she *could* praise Jesus. She more easily
related to Him. Jesus spent time reaching out to the hurting; He talked to disabled people at the temple; He took a
few minutes to chat with children; and He was always on
the lookout for the underdog. Jesus was sensitive, kind,
and compassionate — and this woman felt drawn to God
the Son. She sensed no condemnation from Him, even
when she stumbled and fell into sin. She prayed solely to
Jesus, opening up all conversations with God with the
name of her Savior.

But then something amazing happened.

She read the first chapter of Hebrews and learned that

Jesus is the exact representation of God. She noticed a cross reference and flipped over to John 1:18: "No one has ever seen God, but God the One and Only, who is at the Father's side, has made him known."

The woman was fascinated. She then realized that *knowing Jesus was the same as knowing the Father.* She had no reason to dread or avoid the Father; she could relate to Him because He and the Son are one and the same.

Maybe in the Old Testament people were afraid to approach God, but Jesus threw wide open the door of access to the Father. That alone should cause us to praise. What freedom. What confidence. We have no reason to shrink away from the Father, and every reason to trust Him and give Him adoration and worship. He invites us into intimacy.

A Step Closer

My friends, the blood of Jesus gives us
courage to enter the most holy place by a
new way that leads to life! And this way
takes us through the curtain that is
Christ himself. We have a great high
priest who is in charge of God's house.
So let's come near God with pure hearts
and a confidence that comes from having
faith.

HEBREWS 10:19–22, CEV

Let's pray. Father, making a path through the Red Sea
was as nothing compared to the path You created
for sinners like me to come into Your presence.
"Come near to God"? O Father, how could it be?
I could have never come near You in a trillion years if You
hadn't created a pathway…through the life and body
of Your own dear Son, who died in my place.
And now, because of Him, because He spilled His blood for
me, I can come before You with confidence and feel Your
embrace. How could I ever praise You enough?
Even so, I do praise You, in my Savior's name.

Day 29

WE JUST NEED HIM

Benjamin, my friend Bonnie's young son, waited patiently for his turn to pray. It was family devotional time, and he listened, head bowed, as someone intoned, "Jesus, we just want to know You better."

When Ben's turn came up, he put forth his petitions,

then closed by saying, "And Jesus, I hope You get to know me better, too."

I can identify with Benjamin's concern. Years ago, while still very young in the faith, I too struggled with some things everybody else seemed to take for granted. Before long, I had cultivated a kind of twisted, upside down view of God's glory.

Sitting in Sunday school, I listened to all of those stories of how Jesus moved among the crowds—how He was always walking here and there with multitudes of people at his heels. I wondered why.

I found myself slightly repelled by the paintings and drawings of Jesus I saw on the walls and in the Bibles. They always made Him look like some sanctimonious saint—you know, someone with His head way up in the clouds.

As a youngster, I fostered the idea that God was on an ego trip, always telling people how wonderful He was. Telling people that they should get to know Him. Calling lots of folks to follow Him. I got the impression that God just had to be worshiped—that somehow He had to have a big crowd of people adoring Him.

Maybe you'd never admit it out loud, but have you ever found yourself thinking thoughts like those? Do you ever feel like God is making a bit much of all this stuff about His glory? Do you ever wonder if all this attention He is getting is simply satisfying His ego? Do you ever question exactly *why* God wants us to get to know Him?

If we're going to wrestle with questions like these, we had better stop using human logic. With God's help, we need to view these mysteries from His perspective. Many years ago, in a book called *A Step Further*, I tried to do that. Suppose you, like God, were the most true, just, pure, lovely, and praiseworthy being in existence. And what if everything else in the universe that had any of these qualities got them from you, as a reflection of yourself. For that matter, suppose that without you, these qualities never existed?

If that were the case, then for anyone around you to improve in any way, they would have to become more like you. For you to ask people to think about these good qualities would be to ask them to think about you. Their ego trips would be wrong, for then they would be centering their thoughts around sin and imperfection. But your "ego trip" would be glorious. Indeed, it would be the only hope for humankind, for your so-called ego trip would revolve around perfection.

So when God asks us to think about Him, He asks us to think about everything that is true, just, pure, lovely, and praiseworthy.... He knows how desperately we need His qualities to become ours.

God knows that the more we get to know Him, the more we will know of life—real life—the life we were created to experience. HE IS LIFE.

He understands that by walking with Him, we will better comprehend what genuine love is all about—how it differs from the tawdry imitations put forward by the world. HE IS LOVE.

By focusing our thoughts on Him, we will grasp more fully His goodness, and be all the better for it. HE IS GOODNESS.

Our minds will begin to blossom as we feed on the truth of His Word—pure truth, unadulterated by prejudice, politics, or impure motives. HE IS TRUTH.

We'll come to see how much we really do depend on Him for everything, from salvation to strength for each day...to the next breath we draw into our lungs.

God wants us to get to know Him intimately—not because He needs our worship, but because we need His strength. It has nothing to do with satisfying His ego but everything to do with our hope of making sense out of life today and finding eternal life in the future.

God's glory, someone has said, is man's highest good. The better we know Him and the closer we draw to Him, the stronger, more joyful, more peaceful our lives will be.

Knowing that, He invites us to draw near.

A Step Closer

"Hear, O my people, and I will warn
you—if you would but listen to me,
O Israel!
You shall have no foreign god
among you; you shall not bow
down to an alien god.
I am the LORD your God,
who brought you up out of Egypt.
Open wide your mouth and I will fill it."

PSALM 81:8–10

Psalm 81 reveals the longing of God's
heart like few other places in Scripture.
Within the lines of this song of Israel,
God groans aloud at the stubborn resistance
and fickle hearts of His people.
You get the picture of a God who longs to
help and defend, who can't wait to pour out His blessings.
Read the psalm, and feel His heart today.
It's a good picture of how the Holy Spirit longs
for us to obey His promptings and draw near to Jesus.

Day 30

STEPPING ON GOD'S HEELS

*L*ike to hike?

No, you don't have to be a back-to-nature zealot or a starry-eyed mountain climber. How about a Sunday amble down a country road…or an October stroll through a park, kicking the leaves?

When I was on my feet, hiking was one of the finest things I could anticipate. And we were blessed having a big state park backed up against our farm. Oh, there were countless streams to follow and trails to explore!

My dad was a great hiker. Even when we were as young as five or six years old, my sisters and I would line up behind him as he led the way. We never knew where we were going, but with my dad in charge, striding out in front of us, we were convinced it would be an adventure.

Because of my excitement to always see what was just around the corner or over the next hill, I was constantly stepping on my dad's heels, bumping into his back every now and then. Not that I dared run ahead of him. I just knew that his trail was hot. He was going places! And as long as I hiked right behind him, I'd be able to keep up and not miss a single thing he wanted to show us.

Funny thing. Seasoned hiker that my father was, he never seemed to get irritated at us girls for following too closely. Even though we occasionally stepped on his heels, or telescoped into his back when he stopped, I think he took delight in our excitement to stay so close...to stick together...to follow him on the trail.

Don't you wish for that kind of excitement when following the Lord Jesus? Wouldn't it be glorious if we could always look at our Christian walk as a great adventure?

Maybe that's why Psalm 119:133 draws me so much. The psalmist writes: "Direct my footsteps according to your word." I like to think I'm on an adventurous journey with Christ as leader. And you know something? I would also want to be the sort of follower who is constantly stepping on the Lord's heels, bumping into His back, excited to see what lies around the next bend or over the next hill.

No, I don't want to detour around God. I don't want to run ahead of Him. (How foolish that would be!) I just want to stay close behind Him in my Christian life. I want to know the trail is fresh. I don't want to miss a thing He might want to point out to me.

"My soul follows close behind You," sang David, "Your right hand upholds me" (Psalm 63:8, NKJV).

And how does our heavenly Father feel about our tagging along so closely? *Delighted.* Nothing could please Him more than when we, His children, desire to stay close. It brings Him great joy when we stick together and follow Him on the trail.

You have made known to me the path of life;
you will fill me with joy in your presence.... You
chart the path ahead of me and tell me where to
stop and rest. (Psalm 16:11, NIV; 139:3, NLT)

So let me ask you again. What do you think about hiking? And for that matter, how do you view the path you are trekking through life?

Would to God that we all could keep stepping on the heels of the Lord Jesus, bumping into His back every once in a while. How wonderful if we could make it our goal to follow Him and His leading that closely.

Today, let's make sure we keep on His heels.

A Step Closer

The steps of a man are established
by the LORD,
And He delights in his way.
When he falls, he will not
be hurled headlong,
Because the LORD is the
One who holds his hand.

PSALM 37:23—24, NASB

I came across a verse recently that really has nothing to do
with following God…it's in another context entirely.
It's from 2 Kings 11:8, where a priest tells a group of soldiers,
"Stay close to the king wherever he goes."
Even so, it's great advice for those of us who seek to follow
Christ. Stay close to the King. Go where He goes.
Stop where He stops. Hurry when He hurries,
and take it slow when He does. To do this, to live this way,
requires a heart that keeps in tune with His all day long.
Resolve to do that today…to the best of your ability.
Stay close to Him, and you'll never lose your way.

Day 31

GOD CHOOSES INTIMACY

*I*ntimate friends share secrets.

I'm a people person, and it just comes naturally to confide in a friend, seek sympathy when I'm hurt, or look for approval if I complete a painting I'm especially pleased with.

Almost everybody engages in those sorts of social bonds. A rainbow of personal dynamics flows between us.

We develop frank habits in our relationships—action and interaction. Even our trustfulness, our eagerness to find some ear for our most sacred secrets, demonstrates that we're people dependent. The satisfaction we find in sharing our hopes and cares and wrongs with those who care about us is a sign we are finite and frail. So very, very human.

God, on the other hand, is a mystery.

He holds back many things to remind us of His unapproachable majesty and perfection. Unlike us, He often remains silent. A silence that tells us He is totally self-sufficient. No matter what you've heard, God doesn't need our help. He doesn't *need* anything. If He so chooses, God can accomplish all of His desires without the slightest cooperation of one of us. "Whom did the LORD consult to enlighten him, and who taught him the right way?" asks the prophet Isaiah. "Who was it that taught him knowledge or showed him the path of understanding?" (Isaiah 40:14).

The answer, of course, is no one.

But here's the marvel. Although God is totally self-sufficient, He *chooses* to become intimate with the men and women He has bought for Himself. He *chooses* to involve Himself in our lives. There's a little verse in Psalm 25 which astounds me every time I think of it.

> The LORD confides in those who fear him;
> he makes his covenant known to them.

v. 14

Other translations say, "The Lord is intimate with those who fear Him." *The Amplified Bible* renders it like this: "The secret of the sweet satisfying companionship of the Lord have they who fear (revere and worship) Him, and He will show them His covenant and reveal to them its deep, inner meaning."

God doesn't need to, but He shares His secrets with me. He gets personal and intimate. He lets down His guard. He draws me into quiet conversation. He invites me into His confidence. *Me!*

The Lord of creation certainly doesn't need little old me. He doesn't require my advice. He doesn't need my attention, emotional support, or listening ear. He can go about His business as though I never existed. (He seemed to manage just fine before I was born.) He doesn't have to stoop so low as to use a broken, earthen vessel such as myself. It is only by His unbelievable grace that He calls my simple labor an actual service to Himself. He permits, even solicits my help.

And to think He would whisper the secrets of His heart into my ear!

But here's the catch. Usually we reserve our intimate secrets and confidences for those with whom we are especially buddy-buddy. Not so with God. God reserves intimacies for those who *fear* Him. Those who hold Him in awe and deep respect. Those who revere His name.

I'm overwhelmed at His great glory, His total self-sufficiency, His holiness and completeness. But I'm even more overwhelmed when I consider that God, by His own choice, makes His covenants known to you and me. Insecure, frail, stumbling you and me.

That's a secret I can hardly keep to myself.

A Step Closer

Then the LORD said, "Shall I hide from
Abraham what I am about to do?"

GENESIS 18:17

The LORD detests a perverse man
but takes the upright into his confidence.

PROVERBS 3:32

*Friendship with God! The Almighty Sovereign of the Universe
taking the likes of you and me into His confidence.
Begin your prayers to God today by praising Him for His
justice—so mighty and merciful—for His white-hot holiness,
for His limitless power. Bow low before Him, even literally
getting down on your face, if you are able. Give Him the
honor due His name. It is this God, this great King,
who chooses to reveal secrets to those who fear Him.*

Conclusion

*A*n artist paints so that people might *see*.

You share beauty, elevate the imagination, inspire and challenge the senses—and seek to do it all without being blatant or obvious. The good artist will let the viewer discover truth for himself.

I think of a recent painting of a horse. As I painted, there were parts on that horse I thought especially attractive—parts I wanted the viewer to notice. Like that nice place where neck turns into chest. Those slender ankles. The tilt of the head.

I thought to myself, *How can I lead the viewer to look at these places without being obvious?*

I noticed the horse's coat was a warm, golden color. What is the opposite of gold? Violet, of course—a cool, dark contrast to the horse's coat.

That's what I'll do. I'll lay this cool violet next to the special places on the horse. That will draw attention without being too conspicuous.

As I worked on the horse's neck, I brushed a hint of violet alongside the gold. When placed alongside each other, these colors, subtle and mysterious, would attract your attention. Artistically, it was a successful attempt to get the viewer to see what I wanted him to see.

Our God is a master artist.

And there are aspects of your life and character— good, quality things—He wants others to notice. So without using blatant tricks or obvious gimmicks, God brings the cool, dark contrast of suffering into your life. That contrast, laid up against the golden character of Christ within you, will draw attention…to Him.

Light against darkness. Beauty against affliction. Joy against sorrow. A sweet, patient spirit against pain and disappointment—major contrasts that have a way of attracting notice. Your life begins to snap with interest. People notice you out of the corner of their eye—are drawn to you—without really understanding why.

They are, in fact, seeing what the Master Artist wants them to observe: Christ in you, highlighted against an opposing force of dark suffering.

He draws you into intimacy with Himself, even in the most difficult, pressure-filled days of your life. Jesus allows you to know Him through the "fellowship of sharing in his sufferings."

Whether He chooses to use dark paint or light, you are the canvas on which He paints glorious truths, sharing beauty and inspiring others.

So that people might see Him.